BTFM

Blue Team Field Manual

ALAN WHITE
BEN CLARK

Version 1, Rel 2

ISBN-13: 978-1541016361
ISBN-10: 154101636X

Technical Editor: Matt Hulse

PREFACE

BTFM Command-Line Syntax:

Notation	Description
#	Generic Linux/*nux shell prompt, sudo may also be used with $
C:\>	Windows Prompt, may require Administrator CMD prompt
PS C:\>	Windows PowerShell
>	Generic prompt, multi OS
<IP ADDRESS>, <PORT>, <USER>, <PASSWORD>, etc.	Requires user determined input and remove <> brackets
-	Caution use of copy/paste with dash/hyphens. en/em/dash ,-,- hyphen -
spaces	Ensure you check spaces and no spaces in commands.

Updates, Edits and Supplement Material:

Ref. http://www.blueteamfieldmanual.com

BTFM is based on the NIST Cybersecurity Framework:

Ref. http://www.nist.gov/cyberframework/

TABLE OF CONTENTS

0 PREPARATION (DOCUMENTATION REVIEW)

KEY DOCUMENTS

- Organization Chart
- Network Diagrams
- Data Flow Diagrams
- Critical Asset, Data and Services List
- Rules of Engagement (ROE) Limitations and Boundaries
- Incident Response Plan
- Business Continuity Plan
- Disaster Recovery Plan
- Required Notification Guidance
- Actions to Date
- Physical Access Requirements
- On call/contracted resources
- Communication Plan
- Authority and Legal Conditions
- Threat Intelligence Summary
- Meetings and Deliverable Reporting Requirements
- Physical Security Plan
- Risk Assessment Decision Matrix
- Data and Info Disclosure Procedures
- Consent to Monitor, Collect and Assess Data
- MOA/MOU/NDA Documents and Requirements

1 IDENTIFY (SCOPE)

SCANNING AND VULNERABILITIES

NMAP

Ping sweep for network:

nmap -sn -PE <IP ADDRESS OR RANGE>

Scan and show open ports:

nmap --open <IP ADDRESS OR RANGE>

Determine open services:

nmap -sV <IP ADDRESS>

Scan two common TCP ports, HTTP and HTTPS:

nmap -p 80,443 <IP ADDRESS OR RANGE>

Scan common UDP port, DNS:

nmap -sU -p 53 <IP ADDRESS OR RANGE>

Scan UDP and TCP together, be verbose on a single host and include optional skip ping:

nmap -v -Pn -sU -sT -p U:53,111,137,T:21-25,80,139,8080 <IP ADDRESS>

NESSUS

Basic Nessus scan:

nessus -q -x -T html <NESSUS SERVER IP ADDRESS> <NESSUS SERVER PORT 1241> <ADMIN ACCOUNT> <ADMIN PASSWORD> <FILE WITH TARGETS>.txt <RESULTS FILE NAME>.html

nessus [-vnh] [-c .rcfile] [-V] [-T <format>]

Batch-mode scan:

nessus -q [-pPS] <HOST> <PORT> <USER NAME> <PASSWORD> <targets-file> <result-file>

Report conversion:

nessus -i in.[nsr|nbe] -o out.[xml|nsr|nbe|html|txt]

Step 1: Install the server, client and plugin packages:

apt-get install openvas-server openvas-client openvas-plugins-base openvas-plugins-dfsg

Step 2: Update the vulnerability database

openvas-nvt-sync

Step 3: Add a user to run the client:

openvas-adduser

Step 4: Login: sysadm

Step 5: Authentication (pass/cert) [pass]: [HIT ENTER]

Step 6: Login password: <PASSWORD>

You will then be asked to add "User rules".

Step 7: Allow this user to scan authorized network by typing:

accept <YOUR IP ADDRESS OR RANGE>

default deny

Step 8: type ctrl-D to exit, and then accept.

Step 9: Start the server:

service openvas-server start

Step 10: Set targets to scan:

Create a text file with a list of hosts/networks to scan.

vi scanme.txt

Step 11: Add one host, network per line:

<IP ADDRESS OR RANGE>

Step 12: Run scan:

openvas-client -q 127.0.0.1 9390 sysadm nsrc+ws scanme.txt openvas-output-.html -T txt -V -x

Step 13: (Optional)run scan with HTML format:

openvas-client -q 127.0.0.1 9390 sysadm nsrc+ws scanme.txt openvas-output.txt -T html -V -x

WINDOWS

NETWORK DISCOVERY

Basic network discovery:

C:\> net view /all

C:\> net view \\<HOST NAME>

Basic ping scan and write output to file:

C:\> for /L %I in (1,1,254) do ping -w 30 -n 1
192.168.1.%I | find "Reply" >> <OUTPUT FILE NAME>.txt

DHCP

Enable DHCP server logging:

C:\> reg add
HKLM\System\CurrentControlSet\Services\DhcpServer\Paramete
rs /v ActivityLogFlag /t REG_DWORD /d 1

Default Location Windows 2003/2008/2012:

C:\> %windir%\System32\Dhcp

DNS

Default location Windows 2003:

C:\> %SystemRoot%\System32\Dns

Default location Windows 2008:

C:\> %SystemRoot%\System32\Winevt\Logs\DNS Server.evtx

Default location of enhanced DNS Windows 2012 R2:

C:\> %SystemRoot%\System32\Winevt\Logs\Microsoft-Windows-
DNSServer%4Analytical.etl

Ref. https://technet.microsoft.com/en-
us/library/cc940779.aspx

Enable DNS Logging:

```
C:\> DNSCmd <DNS SERVER NAME> /config /logLevel 0x8100F331
```

Set log location:

```
C:\> DNSCmd <DNS SERVER NAME> /config /LogFilePath
<PATH TO LOG FILE>
```

Set size of log file:

```
C:\> DNSCmd <DNS SERVER NAME> /config /logfilemaxsize
0xffffffff
```

HASHING

File Checksum Integrity Verifier (FCIV):

Ref. http://support2.microsoft.com/kb/841290

Hash a file:

```
C:\> fciv.exe <FILE TO HASH>
```

Hash all files on C:\ into a database file:

```
C:\> fciv.exe c:\ -r -md5 -xml <FILE NAME>.xml
```

List all hashed files:

```
C:\> fciv.exe -list -sha1 -xml <FILE NAME>.xml
```

Verify previous hashes in db with file system:

```
C:\> fciv.exe -v -sha1 -xml <FILE NAME>.xml
```

Note: May be possible to create a master db and compare to all systems from a cmd line. Fast baseline and difference.

Ref. https://technet.microsoft.com/en-us/library/dn520872.aspx

```
PS C:\> Get-FileHash <FILE TO HASH> | Format-List
```

```
PS C:\> Get-FileHash -algorithm md5 <FILE TO HASH>
```

```
C:\> certutil -hashfile <FILE TO HASH> SHA1
```

```
C:\> certutil -hashfile <FILE TO HASH> MD5
```

NETBIOS

Basic nbtstat scan:

```
C:\> nbtstat -A <IP ADDRESS>
```

Cached NetBIOS info on localhost:

```
C:\> nbtstat -c
```

Script loop scan:

```
C:\> for /L %I in (1,1,254) do nbstat -An 192.168.1.%I
```

USER ACTIVITY

Ref. https://technet.microsoft.com/en-us/sysinternals/psloggedon.aspx

Get users logged on:

```
C:\> psloggedon \\computername
```

Script loop scan:

```
C:\> for /L %i in (1,1,254) do psloggedon \\192.168.1.%i
>> C:\users_output.txt
```

PASSWORDS

Password guessing or checks:

```
# for /f %i in (<PASSWORD FILE NAME>.txt) do @echo %i &
net use \\<TARGET IP ADDRESS> %i /u:<USER NAME> 2>nul &&
pause
```

```
# for /f %i in (<USER NAME FILE>.txt) do @(for /f %j in
(<PASSWORD FILE NAME>.txt) do @echo %i:%j & @net use
\\<TARGET IP ADDRESS> %j /u:%i 2>nul && echo %i:%j >>
success.txt && net use \\<IP ADDRESS> /del)
```

MICROSOFT BASELINE SECURITY ANALYZER (MBSA)

Basic scan of a target IP address:

```
C:\> mbsacli.exe /target <TARGET IP ADDRESS> /n
os+iis+sql+password
```

Basic scan of a target IP range:

```
C:\> mbsacli.exe /r <IP ADDRESS RANGE> /n
os+iis+sql+password
```

Basic scan of a target domain:

```
C:\> mbsacli.exe /d <TARGET DOMAIN> /n os+iis+sql+password
```

Basic scan of a target computer names in text file:

```
C:\> mbsacli.exe /listfile <LISTNAME OF COMPUTER
NAMES>.txt /n os+iis+sql+password
```

ACTIVE DIRECTORY INVENTORY

List all OUs:

```
C:\> dsquery ou DC=<DOMAIN>,DC=<DOMAIN EXTENSION>
```

List of workstations in the domain:

```
C:\> netdom query WORKSTATION
```

List of servers in the domain:

```
C:\> netdom query SERVER
```

List of domain controllers:

```
C:\> netdom query DC
```

List of organizational units under which the specified user can create a machine object:

```
C:\> netdom query OU
```

List of primary domain controller:

```
C:\> netdom query PDC
```

List the domain trusts:

```
C:\> netdom query TRUST
```

Query the domain for the current list of FSMO owners

```
C:\> netdom query FSMO
```

List all computers from Active Directory:

```
C:\> dsquery COMPUTER "OU=servers,DC=<DOMAIN
NAME>,DC=<DOMAIN EXTENSION>" -o rdn -limit 0 >
C:\machines.txt
```

List user accounts inactive longer than 3 weeks:

```
C:\> dsquery user domainroot -inactive 3
```

Find anything (or user) created on date in UTC using timestamp format YYYYMMDDHHMMSS.sZ:

```
C:\> dsquery * -filter "(whenCreated>=20101022083730.0Z)"

C:\> dsquery * -filter
"(&(whenCreated>=20101022083730.0Z)(objectClass=user))"
```

Alt option:

```
C:\> ldifde -d ou=<OU NAME>,dc=<DOMAIN NAME>,dc=<DOMAIN
EXTENSION> -l whencreated, whenchanged -p onelevel -r
"(ObjectCategory=user)" -f <OUTPUT FILENAME>
```

The last logon timestamp format in UTC: YYYYMMDDHHMMSS

Alt option:

```
C:\> dsquery * dc=<DOMAIN NAME>,dc=<DOMAIN EXTENSION> -
filter "(&(objectCategory=Person)

(objectClass=User)(whenCreated>=20151001000000.0Z))"
```

Alt option:

```
C:\> adfind -csv -b dc=<DOMAIN NAME>,dc=<DOMAIN EXTENSION>
-f "(&(objectCategory=Person)

(objectClass=User)(whenCreated>=20151001000000.0Z))"
```

Using PowerShell, dump new Active Directory accounts in last 90 Days:

```
PS C:\> import-module activedirectory

PS C:\> Get-QADUser -CreatedAfter (Get-Date).AddDays(-90)
```

```
PS C:\> Get-ADUser -Filter * -Properties whenCreated |
Where-Object {$_.whenCreated -ge ((Get-Date).AddDays(-
90)).Date}
```

LINUX

NETWORK DISCOVERY

Net view scan:

```
# smbtree -b
# smbtree -D
# smbtree -S
```

View open SMB shares:

```
# smbclient -L <HOST NAME>
# smbstatus
```

Basic ping scan:

```
# for ip in $(seq 1 254); do ping -c 1
192.168.1.$ip>/dev/null; [ $? -eq 0 ] && echo
"192.168.1.$ip UP" || : ; done
```

DHCP

View DHCP lease logs:

Red Hat 3:

```
# cat /var/lib/dhcpd/dhcpd.leases
```

Ubuntu:

```
# grep -Ei 'dhcp' /var/log/syslog.1
```

Ubuntu DHCP logs:

```
# tail -f dhcpd.log
```

DNS

Start DNS logging:

```
# rndc querylog
```

View DNS logs:

```
# tail -f /var/log/messages | grep named
```

HASHING

Hash all executable files in these specified locations:

```
# find /<PATHNAME TO ENUMERATE> -type f -exec md5sum {} >>
md5sums.txt \;

# md5deep -rs / > md5sums.txt
```

NETBIOS

Basic nbtstat scan:

```
# nbtscan <IP ADDRESS OR RANGE>
```

PASSWORDS

Password and username guessing or checks:

```
# while read line; do username=$line; while read line; do
smbclient -L <TARGET IP ADDRESS> -U $username%$line -g -d
0; echo $username:$line;  done<<PASSWORDS>.txt; done<<USER
NAMES>.txt
```

2 PROTECT (DEFEND)

WINDOWS

DISABLE/STOP SERVICES

Get a list of services and disable or stop:

```
C:\> sc query

C:\> sc config "<SERVICE NAME>" start= disabled

C:\> sc stop "<SERVICE NAME>"

C:\> wmic service where name='<SERVICE NAME>' call
ChangeStartmode Disabled
```

HOST SYSTEM FIREWALLS

Show all rules:

```
C:\> netsh advfirewall firewall show rule name=all
```

Set firewall on/off:

```
C:\> netsh advfirewall set currentprofile state on

C:\> netsh advfirewall set currentprofile firewallpolicy
blockinboundalways,allowoutbound

C:\> netsh advfirewall set publicprofile state on

C:\> netsh advfirewall set privateprofile state on

C:\> netsh advfirewall set domainprofile state on

C:\> netsh advfirewall set allprofile state on

C:\> netsh advfirewall set allprofile state off
```

Set firewall rules examples:

```
C:\> netsh advfirewall firewall add rule name="Open Port
80" dir=in action=allow protocol=TCP localport=80

C:\> netsh advfirewall firewall add rule name="My
Application" dir=in action=allow
program="C:\MyApp\MyApp.exe" enable=yes

C:\> netsh advfirewall firewall add rule name="My
Application" dir=in action=allow
```

```
program="C:\MyApp\MyApp.exe" enable=yes
remoteip=157.60.0.1,172.16.0.0/16,LocalSubnet
profile=domain

C:\> netsh advfirewall firewall add rule name="My
Application" dir=in action=allow
program="C:\MyApp\MyApp.exe" enable=yes
remoteip=157.60.0.1,172.16.0.0/16,LocalSubnet
profile=domain

C:\> netsh advfirewall firewall add rule name="My
Application" dir=in action=allow
program="C:\MyApp\MyApp.exe" enable=yes
remoteip=157.60.0.1,172.16.0.0/16,LocalSubnet
profile=private

C:\> netsh advfirewall firewall delete rule name=rule name
program="C:\MyApp\MyApp.exe"

C:\> netsh advfirewall firewall delete rule name=rule name
protocol=udp localport=500

C:\> netsh advfirewall firewall set rule group="remote
desktop" new enable=Yes profile=domain

C:\> netsh advfirewall firewall set rule group="remote
desktop" new enable=No profile=public
```

Setup logging location:

```
C:\> netsh advfirewall set currentprofile logging
C:\<LOCATION>\<FILE NAME>
```

Windows firewall log location and settings:

```
C:\>
more %systemroot%\system32\LogFiles\Firewall\pfirewall.log

C:\> netsh advfirewall set allprofile logging maxfilesize
4096

C:\> netsh advfirewall set allprofile logging
droppedconnections enable

C:\> netsh advfirewall set allprofile logging
allowedconnections enable
```

Display firewall logs:

```
PS C:\> Get-Content
$env:systemroot\system32\LogFiles\Firewall\pfirewall.log
```

PASSWORDS

Change password:

```
C:\> net user <USER NAME> * /domain
C:\> net user <USER NAME> <NEW PASSWORD>
```

Change password remotely:

Ref. https://technet.microsoft.com/en-us/sysinternals/bb897543

```
C:\> pspasswd.exe \\<IP ADDRESS or NAME OF REMOTE
COMPUTER> -u <REMOTE USER NAME> -p <NEW PASSWORD>
```

Change password remotely:

```
PS C:\> pspasswd.exe \\<IP ADDRESS or NAME OF REMOTE
COMPUTER>
```

HOST FILE

Flush DNS of malicious domain/IP:

```
C:\> ipconfig /flushdns
```

Flush NetBios cache of host/IP:

```
C:\> nbtstat -R
```

Check Host file location:

```
C:\> reg query
HKLM\SYSTEM\CurrentControlSet\Services\Tcpip\Parameters /f
DatabasePath
```

Add new malicious domain to hosts file, and route to localhost:

```
C:\> echo 127.0.0.1 <MALICIOUS DOMAIN> >>
C:\Windows\System32\drivers\etc\hosts
```

Check if hosts file is working, by sending ping to 127.0.0.1:

```
C:\> ping <MALICIOUS DOMAIN> -n 1
```

WHITELIST

Use a Proxy Auto Config(PAC) file to create Bad URL or IP List (IE, Firefox, Chrome):

```
function FindProxyForURL(url, host) {
// Send bad DNS name to the proxy
if (dnsDomainIs(host, ".badsite.com"))
return "PROXY http://127.0.0.1:8080";
// Send bad IPs to the proxy
if (isInNet(myIpAddress(), "222.222.222.222",
"255.255.255.0"))
return "PROXY http://127.0.0.1:8080";
// All other traffic bypass proxy
return "DIRECT";
}
```

APPLICATION RESTRICTIONS

AppLocker – Server 2008 R2 or Windows 7 or higher:

Using GUI Wizard configure:

- Executable Rules (.exe, .com)
- DLL Rules (.dll, .ocx)
- Script Rules (.ps1, .bat, .cmd, .vbs, .js)
- Windows Install Rules (.msi, .msp, .mst)

Steps to employ AppLocker (GUI is needed for digital signed app restrictions):

Step 1: Create a new GPO.

Step 2: Right-click on it to edit, and then navigate through Computer Configuration, Policies, Windows Settings,

Security Settings, Application Control Policies and AppLocker.

Click Configure Rule Enforcement.

Step 3: Under Executable Rules, check the Configured box and then make sure Enforce Rules is selected from the drop-down box. Click OK.

Step 4: In the left pane, click Executable Rules.

Step 5: Right-click in the right pane and select Create New Rule.

Step 6: On the Before You Begin screen, click Next.

Step 7: On the Permissions screen, click Next.

Step 8: On the Conditions screen, select the Publisher condition and click Next.

Step 9: Click the Browse button and browse to any executable file on your system. It doesn't matter which.

Step 10: Drag the slider up to Any Publisher and then click Next.

Step 11: Click Next on the Exceptions screen.

Step 12: Name policy, Example "Only run executables that are signed" and click Create.

Step 13: If this is your first time creating an AppLocker policy, Windows will prompt you to create default rule, click Yes.

Step 14: Ensure Application Identity Service is Running.

C:\> net start AppIDSvc

C:\> REG add "HKLM\SYSTEM\CurrentControlSet\services\AppIDSvc" /v Start /t REG_DWORD /d 2 /f

Step 15: Changes require reboot.

C:\ shutdown.exe /r

C:\ shutdown.exe /r /m \\<IP ADDRESS OR COMPUTER NAME> /f

Add the AppLocker cmdlets into PowerShell:

```
PS C:\> import-module AppLocker
```

Gets the file information for all of the executable files and scripts in the directory C:\Windows\System32:

```
PS C:\> Get-AppLockerFileInformation -Directory
C:\Windows\System32\ -Recurse -FileType Exe, Script
```

Create an AppLocker Policy that allow rules for all of the executable files in C:\Windows\System32:

```
PS C:\> Get-ChildItem C:\Windows\System32\*.exe | Get-
AppLockerFileInformation | New-AppLockerPolicy -RuleType
Publisher, Hash -User Everyone -RuleNamePrefix System32
```

Sets the local AppLocker policy to the policy specified in C:\Policy.xml:

```
PS C:\> Set-AppLockerPolicy -XMLPolicy C:\Policy.xml
```

Uses the AppLocker policy in C:\Policy.xml to test whether calc.exe and notepad.exe are allowed to run for users who are members of the Everyone group. If you do not specify a group, the Everyone group is used by default:

```
PS C:\> Test-AppLockerPolicy -XMLPolicy C:\Policy.xml -
Path C:\Windows\System32\calc.exe,
C:\Windows\System32\notepad.exe -User Everyone
```

Review how many times a file would have been blocked from running if rules were enforced:

```
PS C:\> Get-AppLockerFileInformation -EventLog -Logname
"Microsoft-Windows-AppLocker\EXE and DLL" -EventType
Audited -Statistics
```

Creates a new AppLocker policy from the audited events in the local Microsoft-Windows-AppLocker/EXE and DLL event log, applied to <GROUP> and current AppLocker policy will be overwritten:

```
PS C:\> Get-AppLockerFileInformation -EventLog -LogPath
"Microsoft-Windows-AppLocker/EXE and DLL" -EventType
Audited | New-AppLockerPolicy -RuleType Publisher,Hash -
User domain\<GROUP> -IgnoreMissingFileInformation | Set-
AppLockerPolicy -LDAP
"LDAP://<DC>.<DOMAIN>.com/CN={31B2F340-016D-11D2-945F-
00C04FB984F9},CN=Policies,CN=System,DC=<DOMAIN>,DC=com"
```

Export the local AppLocker policy, comparing User's explicitly denied access to run, and output text file:

```
PS C:\> Get-AppLockerPolicy -Local | Test-AppLockerPolicy
-Path C:\Windows\System32\*.exe -User domain\<USER NAME> -
Filter Denied | Format-List -Property Path >
C:\DeniedFiles.txt
```

Export the results of the test to a file for analysis:

```
PS C:\> Get-ChildItem <DirectoryPathtoReview> -Filter
<FileExtensionFilter> -Recurse | Convert-Path | Test-
AppLockerPolicy -XMLPolicy <PathToExportedPolicyFile> -
User <domain\username> -Filter <TypeofRuletoFilterFor> |
Export-CSV <PathToExportResultsTo.CSV>
```

GridView list of any local rules applicable:

```
PS C:\> Get-AppLockerPolicy -Local -Xml | Out-GridView
```

IPSEC

Create a IPSEC Local Security Policy, applied to any connection, any protocol, and using a preshared key:

```
C:\> netsh ipsec static add filter
filterlist=MyIPsecFilter srcaddr=Any dstaddr=Any
protocol=ANY

C:\> netsh ipsec static add filteraction
name=MyIPsecAction action=negotiate

C:\> netsh ipsec static add policy name=MyIPsecPolicy
assign=yes

C:\> netsh ipsec static add rule name=MyIPsecRule
policy=MyIPsecPolicy filterlist=MyIPsecFilter
filteraction=MyIPsecAction conntype=all activate=yes
psk=<PASSWORD>
```

Add rule to allow web browsing port 80(HTTP) and 443(HTTPS) over IPSEC:

```
C:\> netsh ipsec static add filteraction name=Allow
action=permit

C:\> netsh ipsec static add filter filterlist=WebFilter
srcaddr=Any dstaddr=Any protocol=TCP dstport=80
```

28

```
C:\> netsh ipsec static add filter filterlist=WebFilter
srcaddr=Any dstaddr=Any protocol=TCP dstport=443
```

```
C:\> netsh ipsec static add rule name=WebAllow
policy=MyIPsecPolicy filterlist=WebFilter
filteraction=Allow conntype=all activate=yes
psk=<PASSWORD>
```

Shows the IPSEC Local Security Policy with name "MyIPsecPolicy":

```
C:\> netsh ipsec static show policy name=MyIPsecPolicy
```

Stop or Unassign a IPSEC Policy:

```
C:\> netsh ipsec static set policy name=MyIPsecPolicy
```

Create a IPSEC Advance Firewall Rule and Policy and preshared key from and to any connections:

```
C:\> netsh advfirewall consec add rule name="IPSEC"
endpoint1=any endpoint2=any action=requireinrequireout
qmsecmethods=default
```

Require IPSEC preshared key on all outgoing requests:

```
C:\> netsh advfirewall firewall add rule name="IPSEC_Out"
dir=out action=allow enable=yes profile=any localip=any
remoteip=any protocol=any interfacetype=any
security=authenticate
```

Create a rule for web browsing:

```
C:\> netsh advfirewall firewall add rule name="Allow
Outbound Port 80" dir=out localport=80 protocol=TCP
action=allow
```

Create a rule for DNS:

```
C:\> netsh advfirewall firewall add rule name="Allow
Outbound Port 53" dir=out localport=53 protocol=UDP
action=allow
```

Delete ISPEC Rule:

```
C:\> netsh advfirewall firewall delete rule
name="IPSEC_RULE"
```

ACTIVE DIRECTORY (AD) - GROUP POLICY OBJECT (GPO)

Get and force new policies:

```
C:\> gpupdate /force
C:\> gpupdate /sync
```

Audit Success and Failure for user Bob:

```
C:\> auditpol /set /user:bob /category:"Detailed Tracking"
/include /success:enable /failure:enable
```

Create an Organization Unit to move suspected or infected users and machines:

```
C:\> dsadd ou <QUARANTINE BAD OU>
```

Move an active directory user object into NEW GROUP:

```
PS C:\> Move-ADObject 'CN=<USER NAME>,CN=<OLD USER
GROUP>,DC=<OLD DOMAIN>,DC=<OLD EXTENSION>' -TargetPath
'OU=<NEW USER GROUP>,DC=<OLD DOMAIN>,DC=<OLD EXTENSION>'
```

Alt Option:

```
C:\> dsmove "CN=<USER NAME>,OU=<OLD USER OU>,DC=<OLD
DOMAIN>,DC=<OLD EXTENSION>" -newparent OU=<NEW USER
GROUP>,DC=<OLD DOMAIN>,DC=<OLD EXTENSION>
```

STAND ALONE SYSTEM - WITHOUT ACTIVE DIRECTORY (AD)

Disallow running a EXE file:

```
C:\> reg add
"HKCU\Software\Microsoft\Windows\CurrentVersion\Policies\E
xplorer" /v DisallowRun /t REG_DWORD /d "00000001" /f
```

```
C:\> reg add
"HKCU\Software\Microsoft\Windows\CurrentVersion\Policies\E
xplorer\DisallowRun" /v badfile.exe /t REG_SZ /d <BAD FILE
NAME>.exe /f
```

Disable Remote Desktop:

```
C:\> reg add
"HKLM\SYSTEM\CurrentControlSet\Control\Terminal Server" /f
/v fDenyTSConnections /t REG_DWORD /d 1
```

Send NTLMv2 response only/refuse LM and NTLM: (Windows 7 default)

```
C:\> reg add HKLM\SYSTEM\CurrentControlSet\Control\Lsa\ /v
lmcompatibilitylevel /t REG_DWORD /d 5 /f
```

Restrict Anonymous Access:

```
C:\> reg add HKLM\SYSTEM\CurrentControlSet\Control\Lsa /v
restrictanonymous /t REG_DWORD /d 1 /f
```

Disable sticky keys:

```
C:\> reg add "HKCU\Control Panel\Accessibility\StickyKeys"
/v Flags /t REG_SZ /d 506 /f
```

Disable Toggle Keys:

```
C:\> reg add "HKCU\Control Panel\Accessibility\ToggleKeys"
/v Flags /t REG_SZ /d 58 /f
```

Disable Filter Keys:

```
C:\> reg add "HKCU\Control Panel\Accessibility\Keyboard
Response" /v Flags /t REG_SZ /d 122 /f
```

Disable IPV6:

```
C:\> reg add
HKLM\SYSTEM\CurrentControlSet\services\TCPIP6\Parameters
/v DisabledComponents /t REG_DWORD /d 255 /f
```

Disable On-screen Keyboard:

```
C:\> reg add
HKLM\SOFTWARE\Microsoft\Windows\CurrentVersion\Authenticat
ion\LogonUI /f /v ShowTabletKeyboard /t REG_DWORD /d 0
```

Disable Administrative Shares – Workstations:

```
C:\> reg add
HKLM\SYSTEM\CurrentControlSet\Services\LanmanServer\Parame
ters /f /v AutoShareWks /t REG_DWORD /d 0
```

Disable Administrative Shares – Servers

```
C:\> reg add
HKLM\SYSTEM\CurrentControlSet\Services\LanmanServer\Parame
ters /f /v AutoShareServer /t REG_DWORD /d 0
```

Do not allow anonymous enumeration of SAM accounts and shares:

```
C:\> reg add HKLM\SYSTEM\CurrentControlSet\Control\Lsa /v
restrictanonymoussam /t REG_DWORD /d 1 /f
```

Remove Creation of Hashes Used to Pass the Hash Attack (Requires password reset and reboot to purge old hashes):

```
C:\> reg add HKLM\SYSTEM\CurrentControlSet\Control\Lsa /f
/v NoLMHash /t REG_DWORD /d 1
```

To Disable Registry Editor: (High Risk)

```
C:\> reg add
HKCU\Software\Microsoft\Windows\CurrentVersion\Policies\Sy
stem /v DisableRegistryTools /t REG_DWORD /d 1 /f
```

Disable IE Password Cache:

```
C:\> reg add
"HKCU\Software\Microsoft\Windows\CurrentVersion\Internet
Settings" /v DisablePasswordCaching /t REG_DWORD /d 1 /f
```

Disable CMD prompt:

```
C:\> reg add
HKCU\Software\Policies\Microsoft\Windows\System /v
DisableCMD /t REG_DWORD /d 1 /f
```

Disable Admin credentials cache on host when using RDP:

```
C:\> reg add HKLM\System\CurrentControlSet\Control\Lsa /v
DisableRestrictedAdmin /t REG_DWORD /d 0 /f
```

Do not process the run once list:

```
C:\> reg add
HKLM\Software\Microsoft\Windows\CurrentVersion\Policies\Ex
plorer /v DisableLocalMachineRunOnce /t REG_DWORD /d 1
```

```
C:\> reg add
HKCU\Software\Microsoft\Windows\CurrentVersion\Policies\Ex
plorer /v DisableLocalMachineRunOnce /t REG_DWORD /d 1
```

Require User Access Control (UAC) Permission:

```
C:\> reg add
HKLM\SOFTWARE\Microsoft\Windows\CurrentVersion\Policies\Sy
stem /v EnableLUA /t REG_DWORD /d 1 /f
```

Change password at next logon:

```
PS C:\> Set-ADAccountPassword <USER> -NewPassword $newpwd
-Reset -PassThru | Set-ADuser -ChangePasswordAtLogon $True
```

Change password at next logon for OU Group:

```
PS C:\> Get-ADuser -filter "department -eq '<OU GROUP>' -
AND enabled -eq 'True'" | Set-ADuser -
ChangePasswordAtLogon $True
```

Enabled Firewall logging:

```
C:\> netsh firewall set logging droppedpackets connections
= enable
```

LINUX

DISABLE/STOP SERVICES

Services information:

service --status-all

ps -ef

ps -aux

Get a list of upstart jobs:

initctl list

Example of start, stop, restarting a service in Ubuntu:

/etc/init.d/apache2 start

/etc/init.d/apache2 restart

/etc/init.d/apache2 stop (stops only until reboot)

service mysql start

service mysql restart

service mysql stop (stops only until reboot)

List all Upstart services:

ls /etc/init/*.conf

Show if a program is managed by upstart and the process ID:

status ssh

If not managed by upstart:

update-rc.d apache2 disable

service apache2 stop

Disable service using systemctl:

systemctl list-units -all --type service

systemctl disable <SERVICE NAME>

Export existing iptables firewall rules:

```
# iptables-save > firewall.out
```

Edit firewall rules and chains in firewall.out and save the file:

```
# vi firewall.out
```

Apply iptables:

```
# iptables-restore < firewall.out
```

Example iptables commands (IP, IP Range, Port Blocks):

```
# iptables -A INPUT -s 10.10.10.10 -j DROP

# iptables -A INPUT -s 10.10.10.0/24 -j DROP

# iptables -A INPUT -p tcp --dport ssh -s 10.10.10.10 -j DROP

# iptables -A INPUT -p tcp --dport ssh -j DROP
```

Block all connections:

```
# iptables-policy INPUT DROP

# iptables-policy OUTPUT DROP

# iptables-policy FORWARD DROP
```

Log all denied iptables rules:

```
# iptables -I INPUT 5 -m limit --limit 5/min -j LOG --log-prefix "iptables denied: " --log-level 7
```

Save all current iptables rules:

Ubuntu:

```
# /etc/init.d/iptables save

# /sbin/service iptables save
```

RedHat / CentOS:

```
# /etc/init.d/iptables save

# /sbin/iptables-save
```

List all current iptables rules:

```
# iptables -L
```

Flush all current iptables rules:

iptables -F

Start/Stop iptables service:

service iptables start

service iptables stop

Start/Stop ufw service:

ufw enable

ufw disable

Start/Stop ufw logging:

ufw logging on

ufw logging off

Backup all current ufw rules:

cp /lib/ufw/{user.rules,user6.rules} /<BACKUP LOCATION>

cp /lib/ufw/{user.rules,user6.rules} ./

Example uncomplicated firewall (ufw) Commands (IP, IP range, Port blocks):

ufw status verbose

ufw delete <RULE #>

ufw allow for <IP ADDRESS>

ufw allow all 80/tcp

ufw allow all ssh

ufw deny from <BAD IP ADDRESS> proto udp to any port 443

PASSWORDS

Change password:

$ passwd (For current user)

$ passwd bob (For user Bob)

$ sudo su passwd (For root)

HOST FILE

Add new malicious domain to hosts file, and route to localhost:

```
# echo 127.0.0.1 <MALICIOUS DOMAIN> >> /etc/hosts
```

Check if hosts file is working, by sending ping to 127.0.0.1:

```
# ping -c 1 <MALICIOUS DOMAIN>
```

Ubuntu/Debian DNS cache flush:

```
# /etc/init.d/dns-clean start
```

Flush nscd DNS cache four ways:

```
# /etc/init.d/nscd restart
# service nscd restart
# service nscd reload
# nscd -i hosts
```

Flush dnsmasq DNS cache:

```
# /etc/init.d/dnsmasq restart
```


WHITELIST

Use a Proxy Auto Config(PAC) file to create bad URL or IP List:

```
function FindProxyForURL(url, host) {

// Send bad DNS name to the proxy

if (dnsDomainIs(host, ".badsite.com"))

return "PROXY http://127.0.0.1:8080";

// Send bad IPs to the proxy

if (isInNet(myIpAddress(), "222.222.222.222", "255.255.255.0"))

return "PROXY http://127.0.0.1:8080";

// All other traffic bypass proxy

return "DIRECT";

}
```

IPSEC

Allow firewall to pass IPSEC traffic:

```
# iptables -A INPUT -p esp -j ACCEPT

# iptables -A INPUT -p ah -j ACCEPT

# iptables -A INPUT -p udp --dport 500 -j ACCEPT

# iptables -A INPUT -p udp --dport 4500 -j ACCEPT
```

Pass IPSEC traffic:

Step 1: Install Racoon utility on <HOST1 IP ADDRESS> and <HOST2 IP ADDRESS> to enable IPSEC tunnel in Ubuntu.

```
# apt-get install racoon
```

Step 2: Choose direct then edit /etc/ipsec-tools.conf on <HOST1 IP ADDRESS> and <HOST2 IP ADDRESS>.

```
flush;

spdflush;

spdadd <HOST1 IP ADDRESS> <HOST2 IP ADDRESS> any -P out ipsec

    esp/transport//require;

spdadd <HOST2 IP ADDRESS> <HOST1 IP ADDRESS> any -P in ipsec

    esp/transport//require;
```

Step 3: Edit /etc/racoon/racoon.conf on <HOST1 IP ADDRESS> and <HOST2 IP ADDRESS>.

```
log notify;

path pre_shared_key "/etc/racoon/psk.txt";

path certificate "/etc/racoon/certs";

remote anonymous {

        exchange_mode main,aggressive;

        proposal {

                encryption_algorithm aes_256;

                hash_algorithm sha256;

                authentication_method pre_shared_key;
```

```
                dh_group modp1024;
        }
        generate_policy off;
}
sainfo anonymous{
        pfs_group 2;
        encryption_algorithm aes_256;
        authentication_algorithm hmac_sha256;
        compression_algorithm deflate;
}
```

Step 4: Add preshared key to both hosts.

On HOST1:

echo <HOST2 IP ADDRESS> <PRESHARED PASSWORD>
>>/etc/racoon/psk.txt

On HOST2:

echo <HOST1 IP ADDRESS> <PRESHARED PASSWORD>
>>/etc/racoon/psk.txt

Step 5: Restart service on both systems.

service setkey restart

Check security associations, configuration and polices:

setkey −D

setkey −DP

3 DETECT (Visibility)

TCPDUMP

View ASCII (-A) or HEX (-X) traffic:

```
# tcpdump -A
```

```
# tcpdump -X
```

View traffic with timestamps and don't convert addresses and be verbose:

```
# tcpdump -tttt -n -vv
```

Find top talkers after 1000 packets (Potential DDoS):

```
# tcpdump -nn -c 1000 |awk '{print $3}' | cut -d. -f1-4 |
sort -n | uniq -c | sort -nr
```

Capture traffic on any interface from a target host and specific port and output to a file:

```
# tcpdump -w <FILENAME>.pcap -i any dst <TARGET IP
ADDRESS> and port 80
```

View traffic only between two hosts:

```
# tcpdump host 10.0.0.1 && host 10.0.0.2
```

View all traffic except from a net or a host:

```
# tcpdump not net 10.10 && not host 192.168.1.2
```

View host and either of two other hosts:

```
# tcpdump host 10.10.10.10 && \(10.10.10.20 or
10.10.10.30\)
```

Save pcap file on rotating size:

```
# tcpdump -n -s65535 -C 1000 -w '%host_%Y-%m-
%d_%H:%M:%S.pcap'
```

Get throughput:

```
# tcpdump -w - |pv -bert >/dev/null
```

Grab traffic that contains the word pass:

```
# tcpdump -n -A -s0 | grep pass
```

Grab many clear text protocol passwords:

```
# tcpdump -n -A -s0 port http or port ftp or port smtp or
port imap or port pop3 | egrep -i
'pass=|pwd=|log=|login=|user=|username=|pw=|passw=|passwd=
|password=|pass:|user:|username:|password:|login:|pass
|user ' --color=auto --line-buffered -B20
```

Save pcap file to a remote host:

```
# tcpdump -w - | ssh <REMOTE HOST ADDRESS> -p 50005 "cat -
> /tmp/remotecapture.pcap"
```

Filter out ipv6 traffic:

```
# tcpdump not ip6
```

Filter out ipv4 traffic:

```
# tcpdump ip6
```

**Script to capture multiple interface tcpdumps to files
rotating every hour:**

```
#!/bin/bash

tcpdump -pni any -s65535 -G 3600 -w any%Y-%m-
%d_%H:%M:%S.pcap
```

**Script to move multiple tcpdump files to alternate
location:**

```
#!/bin/bash

while true; do

sleep 1;

rsync -azvr -progress <USER NAME>@<IP ADDRESS>:<TRAFFIC
DIRECTORY>/. <DESTINATION DIRECTORY/.

done
```

Look for suspicious and self-signed SSL certificates:

```
# tcpdump -s 1500 -A '(tcp[((tcp[12:1] & 0xf0) >> 2)+5:1]
= 0x01) and (tcp[((tcp[12:1] & 0xf0) >> 2):1] = 0x16)'
```

Get SSL Certificate:

```
# openssl s_client -connect <URL>:443
```

```
# openssl s_client -connect <SITE>:443 </dev/null
2>/dev/null | sed -ne '/-BEGIN CERTIFICATE-/,/-END
CERTIFICATE-/p' > <CERT>.pem
```

Examine and verify the certificate and check for Self-Signed:

```
# openssl x509 -text -in <CERT>.pem
```

```
# openssl x509 -in <CERT>.pem -noout -issuer -subject -
startdate -enddate -fingerprint
```

```
# openssl verify <CERT>.pem
```

Extract Certificate Server Name:

```
# tshark -nr <PCAP FILE NAME> -Y
"ssl.handshake.ciphersuites" -Vx| grep "Server Name:" |
sort | uniq -c | sort -r
```

Extract Certificate info for analysis:

```
# ssldump -Nr <FILE NAME>.pcap | awk 'BEGIN {c=0;} { if
($0 ~ /^[ ]+Certificate$/) {c=1; print
"========================================";} if ($0 !~ /^
+/ ) {c=0;} if (c==1) print $0; }'
```


TSHARK

Get list of network interfaces:

```
> tshark -D
```

Listen on multiple network interfaces:

```
> tshark -i eth1 -i eth2 -i eth3
```

Save to pcap and disable name resolution:

```
> tshark -nn -w <FILE NAME>.pcap
```

Get absolute date and time stamp:

```
> tshark -t a
```

Get arp or icmp traffic:

```
> tshark arp or icmp
```

Not ARP and not UDP:

```
> tshark not arp and not (udp.port == 53)
```

Capture traffic between to [hosts] and/or [nets]:

> tshark "host <HOST 1> && host <HOST 2>"

> tshark −n "net <NET 1> && net <NET 2>"

Filter just host and IPs (or not your IP):

> tshark −r <FILE NAME>.pcap −q −z hosts,ipv4

> tshark not host <YOUR IP ADDRESS>

Replay a pcap file:

> tshark −r <FILE NAME>.pcap

Replay a pcap and just grab hosts and IPs:

> tshark −r <FILE NAME>.pcap −q −z hosts

Setup a capture session(duration=60sec):

> tshark −n −a files:10 −a filesize:100 −a duration:60 −w <FILE NAME>.pcap

Grab src/dst IPs only:

> tshark −n −e ip.src −e ip.dst −T fields −E separator=, − R ip

Grab IP of src DNS and DNS query:

> tshark −n −e ip.src −e dns.qry.name −E separator=';' −T fields port 53

Grab HTTP URL host and request:

> tshark −R http.request −T fields −E separator=';' −e http.host −e http.request.uri

Grab just HTTP host requests:

> tshark −n −R http.request −T fields −e http.host

Grab top talkers by IP dst:

> tshark −n −c 150 | awk '{print $4}' | sort −n | uniq −c | sort −nr

Grab top stats of protocols:

```
> tshark -q -z io,phs -r <FILE NAME>.pcap

> tshark -r <PCAP FILE>.cap -R http.request -T fields -e
http.host -e http.request.uri |sed -e 's/?.*$//' | sed -e
's#^(.*)t(.*)$#http://12#' | sort | uniq -c | sort -rn |
head

> tshark -n -c 100 -e ip.src -R "dns.flags.response eq 1"
-T fields port 53

> tshark -n -e http.request.uri -R http.request -T fields
| grep exe

> tshark -n -c 1000 -e http.host -R http.request -T fields
port 80 | sort | uniq -c | sort -r
```

SNORT

Run test on snort config file:

```
# snort -T -c /<PATH TO SNORT>/snort/snort.conf
```

Use snort(v=verbose,d=dump packet payload):

```
# snort -dv -r <LOG FILE NAME>.log
```

Replay a log file and match icmp traffic:

```
# snort -dvr packet.log icmp
```

Logs in ASCII:

```
# snort -K ascii -l <LOG DIRECTORY>
```

Logs in binary:

```
# snort -l <LOG DIRECTORY>
```

Send events to console:

```
# snort -q -A console -i eth0 -c /etc/snort/snort.conf

# snort -c snort.conf -l /tmp/so/console -A console
```

Create a single snort rule and save:

```
# echo alert any any <SNORT RULE> > one.rule
```

Test single rule:

```
# snort -T -c one.rule
```

Run single rule and output to console and logs dir:

```
# mkdir ./logs
```

```
# snort -vd -c one.rule -r <PCAP FILE NAME>.pcap -A
console -l logs
```

NETWORK CAPTURE (PCAP) TOOLS

EDITCAP

Use to edit a pcap file (split into 1000 packets):

> editcap −F pcap −c 1000 orignal.pcap out_split.pcap

Use to edit a pcap file (split into 1 hour each packets):

> editcap −F pcap −t+3600 orignal.pcap out_split.pcap

MERGECAP

Use to merge multiple pcap files:

> mergecap −w merged_cap.pcap cap1.pcap cap2.pcap
cap3.pcap

HONEY TECHNIQUES

WINDOWS

Honey Ports Windows:

Ref. https://code.google.com/archive/p/honeyports/

Step 1: Create new TCP Firewall Block rule on anything connecting on port 3333:

```
C:\> echo @echo off for /L %%i in (1,1,1) do @for /f
"tokens=3" %%j in ('netstat -nao ^| find ^":3333^"')
do@for /f "tokens=1 delims=:" %%k in ("%%j") do netsh
advfirewall firewall add rulename="HONEY TOKEN RULE"
dir=in remoteip=%%k localport=any protocol=TCP
action=block >> <BATCH FILE NAME>.bat
```

Step 2: Run Batch Script

```
C:\> <BATCH FILE NAME>.bat
```

Windows Honey Ports PowerShell Script:

Ref.
https://github.com/Pwdrkeg/honeyport/blob/master/honeyport
.ps1

Step 1: Download PowerShell Script

```
C:\> "%ProgramFiles%\Internet Explorer\iexplore.exe"
https://github.com/Pwdrkeg/honeyport/blob/master/honeyport
.ps1
```

Step 2: Run PowerShell Script

```
C:\> honeyport.ps1
```

Honey Hashes for Windows (Also for Detecting Mimikatz Use):

Ref.
https://isc.sans.edu/forums/diary/Detecting+Mimikatz+Use+O
n+Your+Network/19311/

Step 1: Create Fake Honey Hash. Note enter a fake password and keep command prompts open to keep password in memory

```
C:\> runas /user:yourdomain.com\fakeadministratoraccount
/netonly cmd.exe
```

Step 2: Query for Remote Access Attempts

```
C:\> wevtutil qe System /q:"*[System [(EventID=20274)]]"
/f:text /rd:true /c:1 /r:remotecomputername
```

Step 3: Query for Failed Login Attempts

```
C:\> wevtutil qe Security /q:"*[System[(EventID=4624 or
EventID=4625)]]" /f:text /rd:true /c:5
/r:remotecomputername
```

Step 4: (Optional) Run queries in infinite loop with 30s
pause

```
C:\> for /L %i in (1,0,2) do (Insert Step 2) & (Insert
Step 3) & timeout 30
```


LINUX

Honey Ports Linux:

Ref. http://securityweekly.com/wp-
content/uploads/2013/06/howtogetabetterpentest.pdf

Step 1: Run a while loop to create TCP Firewall rules to
block any hosts connecting on port 2222

```
# while [ 1 ] ; echo "started" ; do IP=`nc -v -l -p 2222
2>&1 1> /dev/null | grep from | cut -d[ -f 3 | cut -d] -f
1`; iptables -A INPUT -p tcp -s ${IP} -j DROP ; done
```

Linux Honey Ports Python Script:

Ref.
https://github.com/gchetrick/honeyports/blob/master/honeyp
orts-0.5.py

Step 1: Download Python Script

```
# wget
https://github.com/gchetrick/honeyports/blob/master/honeyp
orts-0.5.py
```

Step 2: Run Python Script

```
# python honeyports-0.5.py -p <CHOOSE AN OPEN PORT> -h
<HOST IP ADDRESS>
```

Detect rogue scanning with Labrea Tarpit:

```
# apt-get install labrea
# labrea -z -s -o -b -v -i eth0 2>&1| tee -a log.txt
```

NETCAT

Use netcat to listen for scanning threats:

```
> nc -v -k -l 80
> nc -v -k -l 443
> nc -v -k -l 3389
```

PASSIVE DNS MONITORING

Use dnstop to monitor DNS requests at any sniffer location:

```
# apt-get update
# apt-get install dnstop
# dnstop -l 3 <INTERFACE NAME>
```

Step 1: Hit 2 key to show query names

Use dnstop to monitor DNS requests from a pcap file:

```
# dnstop -l 3 <PCAP FILE NAME> | <OUTPUT FILE NAME>.txt
```

LOG AUDITING

WINDOWS

Increase Log size to support increased auditing:

```
C:\> reg add
HKLM\Software\Policies\Microsoft\Windows\EventLog\Applicat
ion /v MaxSize /t REG_DWORD /d 0x19000
```

```
C:\> reg add
HKLM\Software\Policies\Microsoft\Windows\EventLog\Security
/v MaxSize /t REG_DWORD /d 0x64000
```

```
C:\> reg add
HKLM\Software\Policies\Microsoft\Windows\EventLog\System
/v MaxSize /t REG_DWORD /d 0x19000
```

Check settings of Security log:

```
C:\> wevtutil gl Security
```

Check settings of audit policies:

```
C:\> auditpol /get /category:*
```

Set Log Auditing on for Success and/or Failure on All Categories:

```
C:\> auditpol /set /category:* /success:enable
/failure:enable
```

Set Log Auditing on for Success and/or Failure on Subcategories:

```
C:\> auditpol /set /subcategory:"Detailed File Share"
/success:enable /failure:enable
```

```
C:\> auditpol /set /subcategory:"File System"
/success:enable /failure:enable
```

```
C:\> auditpol /set /subcategory:"Security System
Extension" /success:enable /failure:enable
```

```
C:\> auditpol /set /subcategory:"System Integrity"
/success:enable /failure:enable
```

```
C:\> auditpol /set /subcategory:"Security State Change"
/success:enable /failure:enable
```

```
C:\> auditpol /set /subcategory:"Other System Events"
/success:enable /failure:enable

C:\> auditpol /set /subcategory:"System Integrity"
/success:enable /failure:enable

C:\> auditpol /set /subcategory:"Logon" /success:enable
/failure:enable

C:\> auditpol /set /subcategory:"Logoff" /success:enable
/failure:enable

C:\> auditpol /set /subcategory:"Account Lockout"
/success:enable /failure:enable

C:\> auditpol /set /subcategory:"Other Logon/Logoff
Events" /success:enable /failure:enable

C:\> auditpol /set /subcategory:"Network Policy Server"
/success:enable /failure:enable

C:\> auditpol /set /subcategory:"Registry" /success:enable
/failure:enable

C:\> auditpol /set /subcategory:"SAM" /success:enable
/failure:enable

C:\> auditpol /set /subcategory:"Certification Services"
/success:enable /failure:enable

C:\> auditpol /set /subcategory:"Application Generated"
/success:enable /failure:enable

C:\> auditpol /set /subcategory:"Handle Manipulation"
/success:enable /failure:enable

C:\> auditpol /set /subcategory:"File Share"
/success:enable /failure:enable

C:\> auditpol /set /subcategory:"Filtering Platform Packet
Drop" /success:enable /failure:enable

C:\> auditpol /set /subcategory:"Filtering Platform
Connection" /success:enable /failure:enable

C:\> auditpol /set /subcategory:"Other Object Access
Events" /success:enable /failure:enable

C:\> auditpol /set /subcategory:"Detailed File Share"
/success:enable /failure:enable
```

```
C:\> auditpol /set /subcategory:"Sensitive Privilege Use"
/success:enable /failure:enable

C:\> auditpol /set /subcategory:"Non Sensitive Privilege
Use" /success:enable /failure:enable

C:\> auditpol /set /subcategory:"Other Privilege Use
Events" /success:enable /failure:enable

C:\> auditpol /set /subcategory:"Process Termination"
/success:enable /failure:enable

C:\> auditpol /set /subcategory:"DPAPI Activity"
/success:enable /failure:enable

C:\> auditpol /set /subcategory:"RPC Events"
/success:enable /failure:enable

C:\> auditpol /set /subcategory:"Process Creation"
/success:enable /failure:enable

C:\> auditpol /set /subcategory:"Audit Policy Change"
/success:enable /failure:enable

C:\> auditpol /set /subcategory:"Authentication Policy
Change" /success:enable /failure:enable

C:\> auditpol /set /subcategory:"Authorization Policy
Change" /success:enable /failure:enable

C:\> auditpol /set /subcategory:"MPSSVC Rule-Level Policy
Change" /success:enable /failure:enable

C:\> auditpol /set /subcategory:"Filtering Platform Policy
Change" /success:enable /failure:enable

C:\> auditpol /set /subcategory:"Other Policy Change
Events" /success:enable /failure:enable

C:\> auditpol /set /subcategory:"User Account Management"
/success:enable /failure:enable

C:\> auditpol /set /subcategory:"Computer Account
Management" /success:enable /failure:enable

C:\> auditpol /set /subcategory:"Security Group
Management" /success:enable /failure:enable

C:\> auditpol /set /subcategory:"Distribution Group
Management" /success:enable /failure:enable
```

```
C:\> auditpol /set /subcategory:"Application Group
Management" /success:enable /failure:enable

C:\> auditpol /set /subcategory:"Other Account Management
Events" /success:enable /failure:enable

C:\> auditpol /set /subcategory:"Directory Service
Changes" /success:enable /failure:enable

C:\> auditpol /set /subcategory:"Directory Service
Replication" /success:enable /failure:enable

C:\> auditpol /set /subcategory:"Detailed Directory
Service Replication" /success:enable /failure:enable

C:\> auditpol /set /subcategory:"Directory Service Access"
/success:enable /failure:enable

C:\> auditpol /set /subcategory:"Kerberos Service Ticket
Operations" /success:enable /failure:enable

C:\> auditpol /set /subcategory:"Other Account Logon
Events" /success:enable /failure:enable

C:\> auditpol /set /subcategory:"Kerberos Authentication
Service" /success:enable /failure:enable

C:\> auditpol /set /subcategory:"Credential Validation"
/success:enable /failure:enable
```

Check for list of available logs, size, retention limit:

```
PS C:\> Get-EventLog –list
```

**Partial list of Key Security Log Auditing events to
monitor:**

```
PS C:\> Get-EventLog –newest 5 –logname application |
Format-List
```

Show log from remote system:

```
PS C:\> Show-EventLog –computername <SERVER NAME>
```

Get a specific list of events based on Event ID:

```
PS C:\> Get-EventLog Security | ? { $_.EventId –eq 4800}
```

```
PS C:\> Get-WinEvent –FilterHashtable
@{LogName="Security"; ID=4774}
```

Account Logon - Audit Credential Validation Last 14 Days:

```
PS C:\> Get-EventLog Security
4768,4771,4772,4769,4770,4649,4778,4779,4800,4801,4802,480
3,5378,5632,5633 -after ((get-date).addDays(-14))
```

Account - Logon/Logoff:

```
PS C:\> Get-EventLog Security
4625,4634,4647,4624,4625,4648,4675,6272,6273,6274,6275,627
6,6277,6278,6279,6280,4649,4778,4779,4800,4801,4802,4803,5
378,5632,5633,4964 -after ((get-date).addDays(-1))
```

Account Management - Audit Application Group Management:

```
PS C:\> Get-EventLog Security
4783,4784,4785,4786,4787,4788,4789,4790,4741,4742,4743,474
4,4745,4746,4747,4748,4749,4750,4751,4752,4753,4759,4760,4
761,4762,4782,4793,4727,4728,4729,4730,4731,4732,4733,4734
,4735,4737,4754,4755,4756,4757,4758,4764,4720,4722,4723,47
24,4725,4726,4738,4740,4765,4766,4767,4780,4781,4794,5376,
5377 -after ((get-date).addDays(-1))
```

Detailed Tracking - Audit DPAPI Activity, Process Termination, RPC Events:

```
PS C:\> Get-EventLog Security
4692,4693,4694,4695,4689,5712 -after ((get-date).addDays(-
1))
```

Domain Service Access - Audit Directory Service Access:

```
PS C:\> Get-EventLog Security
4662,5136,5137,5138,5139,5141 -after ((get-date).addDays(-
1))
```

Object Access - Audit File Share, File System, SAM, Registry, Certifications:

```
PS C:\> Get-EventLog Security
4671,4691,4698,4699,4700,4701,4702,5148,5149,5888,5889,589
0,4657,5039,4659,4660,4661,4663,4656,4658,4690,4874,4875,4
880,4881,4882,4884,4885,4888,4890,4891,4892,4895,4896,4898
,5145,5140,5142,5143,5144,5168,5140,5142,5143,5144,5168,51
40,5142,5143,5144,5168,4664,4985,5152,5153,5031,5140,5150,
5151,5154,5155,5156,5157,5158,5159 -after ((get-
date).addDays(-1))
```

Policy Change – Audit Policy Change, Microsoft Protection Service, Windows Filtering Platform:

```
PS C:\> Get-EventLog Security
4715,4719,4817,4902,4904,4905,4906,4907,4908,4912,4713,471
6,4717,4718,4739,4864,4865,4866,4867,4704,4705,4706,4707,4
714,4944,4945,4946,4947,4948,4949,4950,4951,4952,4953,4954
,4956,4957,4958,5046,5047,5048,5449,5450,4670 -after
((get-date).addDays(-1))
```

Privilege Use – Audit Non-Sensitive/Sensitive Privilege Use:

```
PS C:\> Get-EventLog Security 4672,4673,4674 -after ((get-date).addDays(-1))
```

System – Audit Security State Change, Security System Extension, System Integrity, System Events:

```
PS C:\> Get-EventLog Security
5024,5025,5027,5028,5029,5030,5032,5033,5034,5035,5037,505
8,5059,6400,6401,6402,6403,6404,6405,6406,6407,4608,4609 ,
4616, 4621, 4610, 4611, 4614,
4622,4697,4612,4615,4618,4816,5038,5056,5057,5060,5061,506
2,6281 -after ((get-date).addDays(-1))
```

Add Microsoft IIS cmdlet:

```
PS C:\> Add-PSSnapin WebAdministration
```

```
PS C:\> Import-Module WebAdministration
```

Get IIS Website info:

```
PS C:\> Get-IISSite
```

Get IIS Log Path Location:

```
PS C:\> (Get-WebConfigurationProperty
'/system.applicationHost/sites/siteDefaults' -Name
'logfile.directory').Value
```

Set variable for IIS Log Path (default path):

```
PS C:\> $LogDirPath = "C:\inetpub\logs\LogFiles\W3SVC1"
```

Get IIS HTTP log file list from Last 7 days:

```
PS C:\> Get-ChildItem -Path
C:\inetpub\logs\LogFiles\w3svc1 -recurse | Where-Object
{$_.lastwritetime -lt (get-date).addDays(-7)}
```

View IIS Logs (Using $LogDirPath variable set above):

```
PS C:\> Get-Content $LogDirPath\*.log |%{$_ -replace
'#Fields: ', ''} |?{$_ -notmatch '^#'} | ConvertFrom-Csv -
Delimiter ' '
```

View IIS Logs:

```
PS C:\> Get-Content <IIS LOG FILE NAME>.log |%{$_ -replace
'#Fields: ', ''} |?{$_ -notmatch '^#'} | ConvertFrom-Csv -
Delimiter ' '
```

Find in IIS logs IP address 192.168.*.* pattern:

```
PS C:\> Select-String -Path $LogDirPath\*.log -Pattern
'192.168.*.*'
```

Find in IIS logs common SQL injection patterns:

```
PS C:\> Select-String -Path $LogDirPath\*.log
'(@@version)|(sqlmap)|(Connect\(\))|(cast\()|(char\()|(bch
ar\()|(sys
databases)|(\(select)|(convert\()|(Connect\())|(count\()|(s
ys objects)'
```


LINUX

Authentication logs in Ubuntu:

```
# tail /var/log/auth.log
# grep -i "fail" /var/log/auth.log
```

User login logs in Ubuntu:

```
# tail /var/
```

Look at samba activity:

```
# grep -i samba /var/log/syslog
```

Look at cron activity:

```
# grep -i cron /var/log/syslog
```

Look at sudo activity:

```
# grep -i sudo /var/log/auth.log
```

Look in Apache Logs for 404 errors:

```
# grep 404 <LOG FILE NAME> | grep -v -E
"favicon.ico|robots.txt"
```

Look at Apache Logs for files requested:

```
# head access_log | awk '{print $7}'
```

Monitor for new created files every 5min:

```
# watch -n 300 -d ls -lR /<WEB DIRECTORY>
```

Look where traffic is coming from:

```
# cat <LOG FILE NAME> | fgrep -v <YOUR DOMAIN> | cut -d\"
-f4 | grep -v ^-
```

Monitor for TCP connections every 5 seconds:

```
# netstat -ac 5 | grep tcp
```

Install audit framework and review syscalls/events:

```
# apt-get install auditd
```

```
# auditctl -a exit,always -S execve
```

```
# ausearch -m execve
```

Get audit report summary:

```
# aureport
```

4 RESPOND (ANALYSIS)

LIVE TRIAGE – WINDOWS

SYSTEM INFORMATION

```
C:\> echo %DATE% %TIME%

C:\> hostname

C:\> systeminfo

C:\> systeminfo | findstr /B /C:"OS Name" /C:"OS Version"

C:\> wmic csproduct get name

C:\> wmic bios get serialnumber

C:\> wmic computersystem list brief

C:\> wmic product get name,version

C:\> echo %PATH%
```
Ref. https://technet.microsoft.com/en-us/sysinternals/psinfo.aspx
```
C:\> psinfo –accepteula –s –h –d
```

USER INFORMATION

```
C:\> whoami

C:\> net users

C:\> net localgroup administrators

C:\> net group administrators

C:\> wmic rdtoggle list

C:\> wmic useraccount list

C:\> wmic group list

C:\> wmic netlogin get name,lastlogon,badpasswordcount

C:\> wmic netclient list brief

C:\> doskey /history > history.txt
```

NETWORK INFORMATION

C:\> netstat -e

C:\> netstat -naob

C:\> netstat -nr

C:\> netstat -vb

C:\> nbtstat -S

C:\> route print

C:\> arp -a

C:\> ipconfig /displaydns

C:\> netsh winhttp show proxy

C:\> ipconfig /allcompartments /all

C:\> netsh wlan show interfaces

C:\> netsh wlan show all

C:\> reg query
"HKLM\SOFTWARE\Microsoft\Windows\CurrentVersion\Internet
Settings\Connections\WinHttpSettings"

C:\> type %SYSTEMROOT%\system32\drivers\etc\hosts

C:\> wmic nicconfig get descriptions,IPaddress,MACaddress

C:\> wmic netuse get
name,username,connectiontype,localname

SERVICE INFORMATION

C:\> at

C:\> tasklist

C:\> tasklist /svc

C:\> tasklist /svc /fi "imagename eq svchost.exe"

C:\> tasklist /svc /fi "pid eq <PID>"

C:\> schtasks

C:\> net start

C:\> sc query

```
C:\> wmic service list brief | findstr "Running"

C:\> wmic service list config

C:\> wmic process list brief

C:\> wmic process list status

C:\> wmic process list memory

C:\> wmic job list brief

PS C:\> Get-Service | Where-Object { $_.Status -eq
"running" }
```

List of all processes and then all loaded modules:

```
PS C:\> Get-Process |select modules|Foreach-
Object{$_.modules}
```

POLICY, PATCH AND SETTINGS INFORMATION

```
C:\> set

C:\> gpresult /r

C:\> gpresult /z > <OUTPUT FILE NAME>.txt

C:\> gpresult /H report.html /F

C:\> wmic qfe
```

List GPO software installed:

```
C:\> reg query "HKLM\Software\Microsoft\Windows\Current
Version\Group Policy\AppMgmt"
```

AUTORUN AND AUTOLOAD INFORMATION

Startup information:

```
C:\> wmic startup list full

C:\> wmic ntdomain list brief
```

View directory contents of startup folder:

```
C:\> dir
"%SystemDrive%\ProgramData\Microsoft\Windows\Start
Menu\Programs\Startup"
```

```
C:\> dir "%SystemDrive%\Documents and Settings\All
Users\Start Menu\Programs\Startup"

C:\> dir %userprofile%\Start Menu\Programs\Startup

C:\> %ProgramFiles%\Startup\

C:\> dir C:\Windows\Start Menu\Programs\startup

C:\> dir
"C:\Users\%username%\AppData\Roaming\Microsoft\Windows\Sta
rt Menu\Programs\Startup"

C:\> dir "C:\ProgramData\Microsoft\Windows\Start
Menu\Programs\Startup"

C:\> dir "%APPDATA%\Microsoft\Windows\Start
Menu\Programs\Startup"

C:\> dir "%ALLUSERSPROFILE%\Microsoft\Windows\Start
Menu\Programs\Startup"

C:\> dir "%ALLUSERSPROFILE%\Start Menu\Programs\Startup"

C:\> type C:\Windows\winstart.bat

C:\> type %windir%\wininit.ini

C:\> type %windir%\win.ini
```

View autoruns, hide Microsoft files:

```
Ref. https://technet.microsoft.com/en-
us/sysinternals/bb963902.aspx

C:\> autorunsc.exe –accepteula –m

C:\> type C:\Autoexec.bat
```

**Show all autorun files, export to csv and check with
VirusTotal:**

```
C:\> autorunsc.exe –accepteula –a –c –i –e –f –l –m –v
```

HKEY_CLASSES_ROOT:

```
C:\> reg query HKCR\Comfile\Shell\Open\Command

C:\> reg query HKCR\Batfile\Shell\Open\Command

C:\> reg query HKCR\htafile\Shell\Open\Command

C:\> reg query HKCR\Exefile\Shell\Open\Command

C:\> reg query HKCR\Exefiles\Shell\Open\Command
```

```
C:\> reg query HKCR\piffile\shell\open\command
```

HKEY_CURRENT_USERS:

```
C:\> reg query "HKCU\Control Panel\Desktop"

C:\> reg query
HKCU\Software\Microsoft\Windows\CurrentVersion\Policies\Ex
plorer\Run

C:\> reg query
HKCU\Software\Microsoft\Windows\CurrentVersion\Run

C:\> reg query
HKCU\Software\Microsoft\Windows\CurrentVersion\Runonce

C:\> reg query
HKCU\Software\Microsoft\Windows\CurrentVersion\RunOnceEx

C:\> reg query
HKCU\Software\Microsoft\Windows\CurrentVersion\RunServices

C:\> reg query
HKCU\Software\Microsoft\Windows\CurrentVersion\RunServices
Once

C:\> reg query
HKCU\Software\Microsoft\Windows\CurrentVersion\Windows\Run

C:\> reg query
HKCU\Software\Microsoft\Windows\CurrentVersion\Windows\Loa
d

C:\> reg query
HKCU\Software\Microsoft\Windows\CurrentVersion\Windows\Scr
ipts

C:\> reg query "HKCU\Software\Microsoft\Windows
NT\CurrentVersion\Windows" /f run

C:\> reg query "HKCU\Software\Microsoft\Windows
NT\CurrentVersion\Windows" /f load

C:\> reg query
HKCU\Software\Microsoft\Windows\CurrentVersion\Policies\Ex
plorer\Run

C:\> reg query
HKCU\Software\Microsoft\Windows\CurrentVersion\Explorer\Re
centDocs
```

```
C:\> reg query
HKCU\Software\Microsoft\Windows\CurrentVersion\Explorer\Co
mDlg32\LastVisitedMRU

C:\> reg query
HKCU\Software\Microsoft\Windows\CurrentVersion\Explorer\Co
mDlg32\OpenSaveMRU

C:\> reg query
HKCU\Software\Microsoft\Windows\CurrentVersion\Explorer\Co
mDlg32\LastVisitedPidlMRU

C:\> reg query
HKCU\Software\Microsoft\Windows\CurrentVersion\Explorer\Co
mDlg32\OpenSavePidlMRU /s

C:\> reg query
HKCU\Software\Microsoft\Windows\CurrentVersion\Explorer\Ru
nMRU

C:\> reg query
"HKCU\Software\Microsoft\Windows\CurrentVersion\Explorer\S
hell Folders"

C:\> reg query
"HKCU\Software\Microsoft\Windows\CurrentVersion\Explorer\U
ser Shell Folders"

C:\> reg query
HKCU\Software\Microsoft\Windows\CurrentVersion\Applets\Reg
Edit /v LastKey

C:\> reg query "HKCU\Software\Microsoft\Internet
Explorer\TypedURLs"

C:\> reg query
"HKCU\Software\Policies\Microsoft\Windows\Control
Panel\Desktop"
```

HKEY_LOCAL_MACHINE:

```
C:\> reg query "HKLM\SOFTWARE\Microsoft\Active
Setup\Installed Components" /s

C:\> reg query
"HKLM\SOFTWARE\Microsoft\Windows\CurrentVersion\explorer\U
ser Shell Folders"
```

```
C:\> reg query
"HKLM\SOFTWARE\Microsoft\Windows\CurrentVersion\explorer\S
hell Folders"

C:\> reg query
HKLM\Software\Microsoft\Windows\CurrentVersion\explorer\Sh
ellExecuteHooks

C:\> reg query
"HKLM\SOFTWARE\Microsoft\Windows\CurrentVersion\Explorer\B
rowser Helper Objects" /s

C:\> reg query
HKLM\SOFTWARE\Microsoft\Windows\CurrentVersion\Policies\Ex
plorer\Run

C:\> reg query
HKLM\SOFTWARE\Microsoft\Windows\CurrentVersion\Run

C:\> reg query
HKLM\SOFTWARE\Microsoft\Windows\CurrentVersion\Runonce

C:\> reg query
HKLM\SOFTWARE\Microsoft\Windows\CurrentVersion\RunOnceEx

C:\> reg query
HKLM\SOFTWARE\Microsoft\Windows\CurrentVersion\RunServices

C:\> reg query
HKLM\SOFTWARE\Microsoft\Windows\CurrentVersion\RunServices
Once

C:\> reg query
HKLM\SOFTWARE\Microsoft\Windows\CurrentVersion\Winlogon\Us
erinit

C:\> reg query
HKLM\SOFTWARE\Microsoft\Windows\CurrentVersion\shellServic
eObjectDelayLoad

C:\> reg query "HKLM\SOFTWARE\Microsoft\Windows
NT\CurrentVersion\Schedule\TaskCache\Tasks" /s

C:\> reg query "HKLM\SOFTWARE\Microsoft\Windows
NT\CurrentVersion\Windows"

C:\> reg query "HKLM\SOFTWARE\Microsoft\Windows
NT\CurrentVersion\Windows" /f AppInit_DLLs

C:\> reg query "HKLM\SOFTWARE\Microsoft\Windows
NT\CurrentVersion\Winlogon" /f Shell
```

```
C:\> reg query "HKLM\SOFTWARE\Microsoft\Windows
NT\CurrentVersion\Winlogon" /f Userinit

C:\> reg query
HKLM\SOFTWARE\Policies\Microsoft\Windows\System\Scripts

C:\> reg query
HKLM\SOFTWARE\Classes\batfile\shell\open\command

C:\> reg query
HKLM\SOFTWARE\Classes\comfile\shell\open\command

C:\> reg query
HKLM\SOFTWARE\Classes\exefile\shell\open\command

C:\> reg query
HKLM\SOFTWARE\Classes\htafile\Shell\Open\Command

C:\> reg query
HKLM\SOFTWARE\Classes\piffile\shell\open\command

C:\> reg query
"HKLM\SOFTWARE\Wow6432Node\Microsoft\Windows\CurrentVersio
n\Explorer\Browser Helper Objects" /s

C:\> reg query
"HKLM\SYSTEM\CurrentControlSet\Control\Session Manager"

C:\> reg query
"HKLM\SYSTEM\CurrentControlSet\Control\Session
Manager\KnownDLLs"

C:\> reg query "HKLM\SYSTEM\ControlSet001\Control\Session
Manager\KnownDLLs"
```

LOGS

Copy event logs:

```
C:\> wevtutil epl Security C:\<BACK UP PATH>\mylogs.evtx

C:\> wevtutil epl System C:\<BACK UP PATH>\mylogs.evtx

C:\> wevtutil epl Application C:\<BACK UP
PATH>\mylogs.evtx
```

Get list of logs remotely:

Ref. https://technet.microsoft.com/en-us/sysinternals/psloglist.aspx

```
C:\> psloglist \\<REMOTE COMPUTER> –accepteula –h 12 –x
```

Clear all logs and start a baseline log to monitor:

```
PS C:\> wevtutil el | Foreach-Object {wevtutil cl "$_"}
```

List log filenames and path location:

```
C:\> wmic nteventlog get path,filename,writeable
```

Take pre-breach log export:

```
PS C:\> wevtutil el | ForEach-Object{Get-EventLog –Log "$_"
| Export-Csv –Path C:\<BASELINE LOG>.csv –Append}
```

Take post breach log export:

```
PS C:\> wevtutil el | ForEach-Object{Get-EventLog –Log "$_"
| Export-Csv –Path C:\<POST BASELINE LOG>.csv –Append}
```

Compare two files baseline and post breach logs:

```
PS C:\> Compare-Object –ReferenceObject $(Get-Content
"C:\<PATH TO FILE>\<ORIGINAL BASELINE LOGS>.txt") –
DifferenceObject $(Get-Content "C:\<PATH TO FILE>\<POST
BASELINE LOGS>.txt") >> <DIFFERENCES LOG>.txt
```

FILES, DRIVES AND SHARES INFORMATION

```
C:\> net use \\<TARGET IP ADDRESS>

C:\> net share

C:\> net session

C:\> wmic volume list brief

C:\> wmic logicaldisk get description,filesystem,name,size

C:\> wmic share get name,path

C:\> wmic diskdrive get interfacetype,mediatype,model

PS:\> Get-ItemProperty –
Path 'HKLM:\SYSTEM\CurrentControlSet\Enum\USBSTOR\*\*' |
Select FriendlyName,ContainerID,HardwareID
```

Find multiple file types or a file:

```
C:\> dir /A /S /T:A *.exe *.dll *.bat *.ps1 *.zip

C:\> dir /A /S /T:A <BAD FILE NAME>.exe
```

Find executable (.exe) files newer than Jan 1, 2017:

```
C:\> forfiles /p C:\ /M *.exe /S /D +1/1/2017 /C "cmd /c
echo @fdate @ftime @path"
```

Find multiple files types using loop:

```
C:\> for %G in (.exe, .dll, .bat, .ps) do forfiles -p "C:"
-m *%G -s -d +1/1/2017 -c "cmd /c echo @fdate @ftime
@path"
```

Search for files newer than date:

```
C:\> forfiles /P C:\ /S /D +1/01/2017 /C "cmd /c echo
@path @fdate"
```

Find large files: (example <20 MB)

```
C:\> forfiles /S /M * /C "cmd /c if @fsize GEQ 2097152
echo @path @fsize"
```

Find files with Alternate Data Streams:

```
Ref. https://technet.microsoft.com/en-
us/sysinternals/streams.aspx

C:\> streams -s <FILE OR DIRECTORY>

C:\> dir /r <FILE OR DIRECTORY>
```

Find files with bad signature into csv:

```
Ref. https://technet.microsoft.com/en-
us/sysinternals/bb897441.aspx

C:\> sigcheck -c -h -s -u -nobanner <FILE OR DIRECTORY> >
<OUTPUT FILENAME>.csv
```

Find and show only unsigned files with bad signature in C:

```
C:\> sigcheck -e -u -vr -s C:\
```

List loaded unsigned DLLs:

```
Ref. https://technet.microsoft.com/en-
us/sysinternals/bb896656.aspx

C:\> listdlls.exe -u
```

```
C:\> listdlls.exe -u <PROCESS NAME OR PID>
```

Run Malware scan (Windows Defender) offline:

Ref. http://windows.microsoft.com/en-us/windows/what-is-windows-defender-offline

```
C:\> MpCmdRun.exe -SignatureUpdate
```

```
C:\> MpCmdRun.exe -Scan
```

Install, monitor and log system activity to the Windows event log including md5 hashing of processes created and monitoring of network connections 64bit:

Ref. https://technet.microsoft.com/en-us/sysinternals/sysmon

```
C:\> sysmon64.exe -i -accepteula -h md5 -n
```

Unistall Sysmon:

```
C:\> sysmon64.exe -u
```

View Sysmon log details:

```
PS C:\> Get-WinEvent -Path
C:\Windows\System32\winevt\Logs\Microsoft-Windows-Sysmon%4Operational.evtx | Format-List *
```

LIVE TRIAGE – LINUX

SYSTEM INFORMATION

```
# uname -a
# uptime
# timedatectl
# mount
# echo $PATH
```

USER INFORMATION

View logged in users:
```
# w
```
Show if a user has ever logged in remotely:
```
# lastlog
# last
```
View failed logins:
```
# faillog -a
```
View local user accounts:
```
# cat /etc/passwd
# cat /etc/shadow
```
View local groups:
```
# cat /etc/group
```
View sudo access:
```
# cat /etc/sudoers
```
View accounts with UID 0:
```
# awk -F: '($3 == "0") {print}' /etc/passwd
# egrep ':0+' /etc/passwd
```

View root authorized SSH key authentications:

```
# cat /root/.ssh/authorized_keys
```

List of files opened by user:

```
# lsof -u <USER NAME>
```

View the root user bash history:

```
# cat /root/.bash_history
```

NETWORK INFORMATION

View network interfaces:

```
# ifconfig
```

View network connections:

```
# netstat -antup
# netstat -plantux
```

View listening ports:

```
# netstat -nap
```

View routes:

```
# route
```

View arp table:

```
# arp -a
```

List of processes listening on ports:

```
# lsof -i
```

SERVICE INFORMATION

View processes:

```
# ps -aux
```

List of load modules:

```
# lsmod
```

List of open files:

```
# lsof
```

List of open files, using the network:

```
# lsof -nPi | cut -f 1 -d " "| uniq | tail -n +2
```

List of open files on specific process:

```
# lsof -c <SERVICE NAME>
```

Get all open files of a specific process ID:

```
# lsof -p <PID>
```

List of unlinked processes running:

```
# lsof +L1
```

Get path of suspicious process PID:

```
# ls -al /proc/<PID>/exe
```

Save file for further malware binary analysis:

```
# cp /proc/<PID>/exe >/<SUSPICIOUS FILE NAME TO SAVE>.elf
```

Monitor logs in real-time:

```
# less +F /var/log/messages
```

List services:

```
# chkconfig --list
```

POLICY, PATCH AND SETTINGS INFORMATION

View pam.d files:

```
# cat /etc/pam.d/common*
```

AUTORUN AND AUTOLOAD INFORMATION:

List cron jobs:

```
# crontab -l
```

List cron jobs by root and other UID 0 accounts:

```
# crontab -u root -l
```

Review for unusual cron jobs:

```
# cat /etc/crontab
# ls /etc/cron.*
```

LOGS

View root user command history:

cat /root/.*history

View last logins:

last

FILES, DRIVES AND SHARES INFORMATION

View disk space:

df -ah

View directory listing for /etc/init.d:

ls -la /etc/init.d

Get more info for a file:

stat -x <FILE NAME>

Identify file type:

file <FILE NAME>

Look for immutable files:

lsattr -R / | grep "\-i-"

View directory listing for /root:

ls -la /root

Look for files recently modified in current directory:

ls -alt | head

Look for world writable files:

find / -xdev -type d \(-perm -0002 -a ! -perm -1000 \) -print

Look for recent created files, in this case newer than Jan 02, 2017:

find / -newermt 2017-01-02q

Look for files with no user owner:

find / -nouser

List all files and attributes:

```
# find / -printf
"%m;%Ax;%AT;%Tx;%TT;%Cx;%CT;%U;%G;%s;%p\n"
```

List for large files over 100MB:

```
# find / -size +100000k -print
```

Look at files in directory by most recent timestamp:(Could be tampered)

```
# ls -alt /<DIRECTORY>| head
```

Get full file information:

```
# stat /<FILE PATH>/<SUSPICIOUS FILE NAME>
```

Review file type:

```
# file /<FILE PATH>/<SUSPICIOUS FILE NAME>
```

Check for rootkits or signs of compromise:

Run unix-privsec-check tool:

```
# wget
https://raw.githubusercontent.com/pentestmonkey/unix-
privesc-check/1_x/unix-privesc-check
```

```
# ./unix-privesc-check > output.txt
```

Run chkrootkit:

```
# apt-get install chkrootkit
```

```
# chkrootkit
```

Run rkhunter:

```
# apt-get install rkhunter
```

```
# rkhunter --update
```

```
# rkhunter -check
```

Run tiger:

```
# apt-get install tiger
```

```
# tiger
```

```
# less /var/log/tiger/security.report.*
```

Run lynis:

```
# apt-get install lynis
```

```
# lynis audit system

# more /var/logs/lynis.log
```

Run Linux Malware Detect (LMD):

```
# wget http://www.rfxn.com/downloads/maldetect-
current.tar.gz

# tar xfz maldetect-current.tar.gz

# cd maldetect-*

# ./install.sh
```

Get LMD updates:

```
# maldet -u
```

Run LMD scan on directory:

```
# maldet -a /<DIRECTORY>
```

MALWARE ANALYSIS

STATIC ANALYSIS BASICS

Mount live Sysinternals tools drive:

```
\\live.sysinternals.com\tools
```

Signature check of DLL, EXE files:

Ref. http://technet.microsoft.com/en-us/sysinternals/bb897441.aspx

```
C:\> sigcheck.exe -u -e C:\<DIRECTORY>
```

Send to VirusTotal:

```
C:\> sigcheck.exe -vt <SUSPICIOUS FILE NAME>
```

Windows PE Analysis:

View Hex and ASCI of PE(EXE or any file), with optional -n first 500 bytes:

```
# hexdump -C -n 500 <SUSPICIOUS FILE NAME>
# od -x <SUSPICIOUS FILE NAME>
# xxd <SUSPICIOUS FILE NAME>
```

In Windows using debug tool (works for .java files too):

```
C:\> debug <SUSPICIOUS FILE NAME>
> -d (just type d and get a page at a time of hex)
> -q (quit debugger)
```

Windows PE analysis:

PE File Compile Date/Time perl script below (Windows PE only script).

Ref. https://www.perl.org/get.html

Ref. http://www.perlmonks.org/bare/?node_id=484287

```
C:\> perl.exe <SCRIPT NAME>.pl <SUSPICIOUS FILE NAME>
#! perl -slw
use strict;
```

```perl
open EXE, '<:raw', $ARGV[0] or die "$ARGV[0] : $!";

my $dos = do{ local $/ = \65536; <EXE> };

die "$ARGV[0] is not a .exe or .dll (sig='${ \substr $dos,
0, 2 }')" unless substr( $dos, 0, 2 ) eq 'MZ';

my $coffoff = 8+ unpack 'x60 V', $dos;

read( EXE, $dos, $coffoff - 65536 + 4, 65536 ) or die $!
if $coffoff > 65536;

my $ts = unpack "x$coffoff V", $dos;

print "$ARGV[0] : ", defined $ts

    ? ( scalar( localtime $ts) || "has unfathomable
timestamp value $ts" )

    : 'has no timestamp';

__END__
```

View strings within PE and optional string length -n option:

Using strings in Linux:

```
# strings -n 10 <SUSPICIOUS FILE NAME>
```

Ref. https://technet.microsoft.com/en-us/sysinternals/strings.aspx

Using strings in Windows:

```
C:\> strings <SUSPICIOUS FILE NAME>
```

Find Malware in memory dump using Volatility and Windows7SPFix64 profile:

Ref. https://github.com/volatilityfoundation/volatility

```
# python vol.py -f <MEMORY DUMP FILE NAME>.raw -
profile=Win7SPFix64 malfind -D /<OUTPUT DUMP DIRECTORY>
```

Find Malware with PID in memory dump using Volatility:

```
# python vol.py -f <MEMORY DUMP FILE NAME>.raw -
profile=Win7SPFix64 malfind -p <PID #> -D /<OUTPUT DUMP
DIRECTORY>
```

Find suspicious processes using Volatility:

```
# python vol.py -f <MEMORY DUMP FILE NAME>.raw -
profile=Win7SPFix64 pslist
```

```
# python vol.py -f <MEMORY DUMP FILE NAME>.raw -
profile=Win7SPFix64 pstree
```

Find suspicious DLLs using Volatility:

```
# python vol.py -f <MEMORY DUMP FILE NAME>.raw -
profile=Win7SPFix64 dlllist
```

```
# python vol.py -f <MEMORY DUMP FILE NAME>.raw -
profile=Win7SPFix64 dlldump -D /<OUTPUT DUMP DIRECTORY>
```

Malware analysis parsing Tool:

Ref. https://github.com/Defense-Cyber-Crime-Center/DC3-MWCP

Install dc3-mwcp tool:

```
# setup.py install
```

Use dc3-mwcp tool to parse suspicious file:

```
# mwcp-tool.py -p <SUSPICIOUS FILE NAME>
```

Install Rekall tool:

Ref. https://github.com/google/rekall

```
# pip install rekall
```

```
# rekal --help
```

Run Rekall against a memory file and extract process list, dlllist, executable dump:

```
# rekal -f <MEMORY FILE>.aff imageinfo
```

```
# rekal -f <MEMORY FILE>.dd pslist
```

```
# rekal -f <MEMORY FILE>.img pslist --pid <PID>
```

```
# rekal -f <MEMORY FILE>.dd dlllist
```

```
# rekal -f <MEMORY FILE> pedump
```

IDENTIFY MALWARE

PROCESS EXPLORER

Ref. https://youtu.be/80vfTA9LrBM

Step 1: Look at running processes by running Process Explorer (GUI) and identify potential indicators of compromise:

- Items with no icon
- Items with no description or company name
- Unsigned Microsoft images (First add Verified Signer column under View tab->Select Columns, then go to Options tab and choose Verify Image Signatures)
- Check all running process hashes in Virus Total (Go to Options tab and select Check VirusTotal.com)
- Suspicious files are in Windows directories or user profile
- Purple items that are packed or compressed
- Items with open TCP/IP endpoints

Step 2: Signature File Check:

(See Sigcheck)

Step 3: Strings Check:

- Right click on suspicious process in Process Explorer and on pop up window choose Strings tab and review for suspicious URLs. Repeat for Image and Memory radio buttons.
- Look for strange URLs in strings

Step 4: DLL View:

- Pop open with Ctrl+D
- Look for suspicious DLLs or services
- Look for no description or no company name
- Look at VirusTotal Results column

Step 5: Stop and Remove Malware:

- Right click and select Suspend for any identified suspicious processes

- Right click and select Terminate Previous Suspended processes

Step 6: Clean up where malicious files Auto start on reboot.

- Launch Autoruns
- Under Options, Check the boxes Verify Code Signatures and Hide Microsoft entries
- Look for suspicious process file from earlier steps on the everything tab and uncheck. Safer to uncheck than delete, in case of error.
- Press F5, to refresh Autoruns, and confirm malicious file has not recreated the malicious entry into the previous unchecked auto start location.

Step 7: Process Monitor

Ref. https://technet.microsoft.com/en-us/sysinternals/processmonitor.aspx

- If malicious activity is still persistent, run Process Monitor.
- Look for newly started process that start soon after terminated from previous steps.

Step 8: Repeat as needed to find all malicious files and process and/or combine with other tools and suites.

FILE HASH ANALYSIS

HASH QUERY

VirusTotal online API query:

Ref. https://www.virustotal.com/en/documentation/public-api/ (Prerequisite: Need a VT API Key)

Send a suspicious hash to VirusTotal using cURL:

```
# curl -v --request POST --url
'https://www.virustotal.com/vtapi/v2/file/report' -d
apikey=<VT API KEY> -d 'resource=<SUSPICIOUS FILE HASH>'
```

Send a suspicious file to VirusTotal using cURL:

```
# curl -v -F 'file=/<PATH TO FILE>/<SUSPICIOUS FILE NAME>'
-F apikey=<VT API KEY>
https://www.virustotal.com/vtapi/v2/file/scan
```

Team Cymru API:

Ref. https://hash.cymru.com, http://totalhash.com

Team Cymru malware hash lookup using whois: (Note: Output is timestamp of last seen and detection rate)

```
# whois -h hash.cymru.com <SUSPICIOUS FILE HASH>
```

HARD DRIVE AND MEMORY ACQUISITION

WINDOWS

Create memory dump remotely:

Ref. http://kromer.pl/malware-analysis/memory-forensics-using-volatility-toolkit-to-extract-malware-samples-from-memory-dump/

Ref. http://sourceforge.net/projects/mdd/

Ref. https://technet.microsoft.com/en-us/sysinternals/psexec.aspx

```
C:\> psexec.exe \\<HOST NAME OR IP ADDRESS> -u
<DOMAIN>\<PRIVILEGED ACCOUNT> -p <PASSWORD> -c mdd_1.3.exe
--o C:\memory.dmp
```

Ref. https://github.com/volatilityfoundation/volatility

Extract EXE/DLL from memory dump:

```
C:\> volatility dlldump -f memory.dmp -D dumps/
```

```
C:\> volatility procmemdump -f memory.dmp -D dumps/
```

Create hard drive image using dc3dd of C:\:

Ref.
https://sourceforge.net/projects/dc3dd/files/dc3dd/7.2%20-%20Windows/

```
C:\> dc3dd.exe if=\\.\c: of=d:\<ATTACHED OR TARGET
DRIVE>\<IMAGE NAME>.dd hash=md5 log=d:\<MOUNTED
LOCATION>\<LOG NAME>.log
```

Create memory dump:

```
# dd if=/dev/fmem of=/tmp/<MEMORY FILE NAME>.dd
```

Create memory dump using LiME:

Ref. https://github.com/504ensicslabs/lime

```
# wget
https://github.com/504ensicsLabs/LiME/archive/master.zip
```

```
# unzip master.zip
```

```
# cd LiME-master/src
```

```
# make
```

```
# cp lime-*.ko /media/=/media/ExternalUSBDriveName/
```

```
# insmod lime-3.13.0-79-generic.ko
"path=/media/ExternalUSBDriveName/<MEMORY DUMP>.lime
format=raw"
```

Make copy of suspicious process using process ID:

```
# cp /proc/<SUSPICIOUS PROCESS ID>/exe /<NEW SAVED
LOCATION>
```

Grab memory core dump of suspicious process:

```
# gcore <PID>
```

Strings on gcore file:

```
# strings gcore.*
```

Create a hard drive/partition copy with log and hash options:

```
# dd if=<INPUT DEVICE> of=<IMAGE FILE NAME>
```

```
# dc3dd if=/dev/<TARGET DRIVE EXAMPLE SDA OR SDA1>
of=/dev/<MOUNTED LOCATION>\<FILE NAME>.img hash=md5
log=/<MOUNTED LOCATION>/<LOG NAME>.log
```

Create a remote hard drive/partition over SSH:

```
# dd if=/dev/<INPUT DEVICE> | ssh <USER NAME>@<DESTINATION
IP ADDRESS> "dd of=<DESTINATION PATH>"
```

Send hard drive image zipped over netcat:

Sending host:

```
# bzip2 -c /dev/<INPUT DEVICE> | nc <DESTINATION IP
ADDRESS> <PICK A PORT>
```

Receiving host:

```
# nc -p <PICK SAME PORT> -l |bzip2 -d | dd of=/dev/sdb
```

Send hard drive image over netcat:

Sending host:

```
# dd if=/dev/<INPUT DEVICE> bs=16M | nc <PORT>
```

Receiving host with Pipe Viewer meter:

```
# nc -p <SAME PORT> -l -vv | pv -r | dd of=/dev/<INPUT
DEVICE> bs=16M
```

5 RECOVER (Remediate)

PATCHING

WINDOWS

Single Hotfix update for Windows 7 or higher:

C:\> wusa.exe C:\<PATH TO HOTFIX>\Windows6.0-KB934307-x86.msu

Set of single hotfix updates for pre-Windows 7 by running a batch script:

```
@echo off
setlocal
set PATHTOFIXES=E:\hotfix
%PATHTOFIXES%\Q123456_w2k_sp4_x86.exe /Z /M
%PATHTOFIXES%\Q123321_w2k_sp4_x86.exe /Z /M
%PATHTOFIXES%\Q123789_w2k_sp4_x86.exe /Z /M
```

To check and update Windows 7 or higher:

C:\> wuauclt.exe /detectnow /updatenow

LINUX

Ubuntu:

Fetch list of available updates:

apt-get update

Strictly upgrade the current packages:

apt-get upgrade

Install updates (new ones):

apt-get dist-upgrade

Red Hat Enterprise Linux 2.1,3,4:

up2date

To update non-interactively:

up2date-nox --update

To install a specific package:

```
# up2date <PACKAGE NAME>
```

To update a specific package:

```
# up2date -u <PACKAGE NAME>
```

Red Hat Enterprise Linux 5:

```
# pup
```

Red Hat Enterprise Linux 6:

```
# yum update
```

To list a specific installed package:

```
# yum list installed <PACKAGE NAME>
```

To install a specific package:

```
# yum install <PACKAGE NAME>
```

To update a specific package:

```
# yum update <PACKAGE NAME>
```

Kali:

```
# apt-get update && apt-get upgrade
```

WINDOWS

Backup GPO Audit Policy to backup file:

C:\> auditpol /backup /file:C\auditpolicy.csv

Restore GPO Audit Policy from backup file:

C:\> auditpol /restore /file:C:\auditpolicy.csv

Backup All GPOs in domain and save to Path:

PS C:\> Backup-Gpo -All -Path \\<SERVER>\<PATH TO BACKUPS>

Restore All GPOs in domain and from backup Path:

PS C:\> Restore-GPO -All -Domain <INSERT DOMAIN NAME> -
Path \\<SERVER>\<PATH TO BACKUPS>

Start Volume Shadow Service:

C:\> net start VSS

List all shadow files and storage:

C:\> vssadmin List ShadowStorage

List all shadow files:

C:\> vssadmin List Shadows

Browse Shadow Copy for files/folders:

C:\> mklink /d c:\<CREATE FOLDER>\<PROVIDE FOLDER NAME BUT
DO NOT CREATE>
\\?\GLOBALROOT\Device\HarddiskVolumeShadowCopy1\

**Revert back to a selected shadow file on Windows Server
and Windows 8:**

C:\> vssadmin revert shadow /shadow={<SHADOW COPY ID>}
/ForceDismount

List a files previous versions history using volrest.exe:

Ref. https://www.microsoft.com/en-us/download/details.aspx?id=17657

```
C:\> "\Program Files (x86)\Windows Resource
Kits\Tools\volrest.exe" "\\localhost\c$\<PATH TO
FILE>\<FILE NAME>"
```

Revert back to a selected previous file version or @GMT file name for specific previous version using volrest.exe:

```
C:\> subst Z: \\localhost\c$\$\<PATH TO FILE>

C:\> "\Program Files (x86)\Windows Resource
Kits\Tools\volrest.exe" "\\localhost\c$\<PATH TO
FILE>\<CURRENT FILE NAME OR @GMT FILE NAME FROM LIST
COMMAND ABOVE>" /R:Z:\

C:\> subst Z: /D
```

Revert back a directory and subdirectory files previous version using volrest.exe:

```
C:\> "\Program Files (x86)\Windows Resource
Kits\Tools\volrest.exe" \\localhost\c$\<PATH TO FOLDER\*.*
/S /r:\\localhost\c$\<PATH TO FOLDER>\
```

Revert back to a selected shadow file on Windows Server and Windows 7 and 10 using wmic:

```
C:\> wmic shadowcopy call create Volume='C:\'
```

Create a shadow copy of volume C on Windows 7 and 10 using PowerShell:

```
PS C:\> (gwmi -list
win32_shadowcopy).Create('C:\','ClientAccessible')
```

Create a shadow copy of volume C on Windows Server 2003 and 2008:

```
C:\> vssadmin create shadow /for=c:
```

Create restore point on Windows:

```
C:\> wmic.exe /Namespace:\\root\default Path SystemRestore
Call CreateRestorePoint "%DATE%", 100, 7
```

Start system restore points on Windows XP:

```
C:\> sc config srservice start= disabled

C:\> reg add
"HKEY_LOCAL_MACHINE\SOFTWARE\Microsoft\Windows
NT\CurrentVersion\SystemRestore" /v DisableSR /t REG_DWORD
/d 1 /f

C:\> net stop srservice
```

Stop system restore points on Windows XP:

```
C:\> sc config srservice start= Auto

C:\> net start srservice

C:\> reg add
"HKEY_LOCAL_MACHINE\SOFTWARE\Microsoft\Windows
NT\CurrentVersion\SystemRestore" /v DisableSR /t REG_DWORD
/d 0 /f
```

List of restore points:

```
PS C:\> Get-ComputerRestorePoint
```

Restore from a specific restore point:

```
PS C:\> Restore-Computer –RestorePoint <RESTORE POINT #> –
Confirm
```

Reset root password in single user mode:

Step 1: Reboot system.

```
# reboot -f
```

Step 2: Press ESC at GRUB screen.

Step 3: Select default entry and then 'e' for edit.

Step 4: Scroll down until, you see a line that starts with linux, linux16 or linuxefi.

Step 5: At end of that line leave a space and add without quote 'rw init=/bin/bash'

Step 6: Press Ctrl-X to reboot.

Step 7: After reboot, should be in single user mode and root, change password.

```
# passwd
```

Step 8: Reboot system.

```
# reboot -f
```

Reinstall a package:

```
# apt-get install --reinstall <COMPROMISED PACKAGE NAME>
```

Reinstall all packages:

```
# apt-get install --reinstall $(dpkg --get-selections
|grep -v deinstall)
```

KILL MALWARE PROCESS

WINDOWS

Malware Removal:

Ref. http://www.gmer.net/

C:\> gmer.exe (GUI)

Kill running malicious file:

C:\> gmer.exe -killfile

C:\WINDOWS\system32\drivers\<MALICIOUS FILENAME>.exe

Kill running process using wmic:

C:\> wmic process <PID> delete

C:\> wmic process where name="<FILENAME.exe>" delete

Kill running malicious file in PowerShell:

PS C:\> Stop-Process -Name <PROCESS NAME>

PS C:\> Stop-Process -ID <PID> -Force

LINUX

Stop a malware process or processes:

kill <MALICIOUS PID>

killall -9 -I <PROCESS NAME>

Change the malware process from execution and move:

chmod -x /usr/sbin/<SUSPICIOUS FILE NAME>

mkdir /home/quarantine/

mv /usr/sbin/<SUSPICIOUS FILE NAME> /home/quarantine/

6 TACTICS (TIPS & TRICKS)

OS CHEATS

WINDOWS

Pipe output to clipboard:

```
C:\> some_command.exe | clip
```

Output clip to file: (Requires PowerShell 5)

```
PS C:\> Get-Clipboard > clip.txt
```

Add time stamps into log file:

```
C:\> echo %DATE% %TIME% >> <TXT LOG>.txt
```

Add/Modify registry value remotely:

```
C:\> reg add \\<REMOTE COMPUTER NAME>\HKLM\Software\<REG
KEY INFO>
```

Get registry value remotely:

```
C:\> reg query \\<REMOTE COMPUTER NAME>\HKLM\Software\<REG
KEY INFO>
```

Test to see if Registry Path exists:

```
PS C:\> Test-Path "HKCU:\Software\Microsoft\<HIVE>"
```

Copy files remotely:

```
C:\> robocopy C:\<SOURCE SHARED FOLDER> \\<DESTINATION
COMPUTER>\<DESTINATION FOLDER> /E
```

Check to see if certain file extensions are in a directory:

```
PS C:\> Test-Path C:\Scripts\Archive\* -include *.ps1,
*.vbs
```

Show contents of a file:

```
C:\> type <FILE NAME>
```

Combine contents of multiple files:

```
C:\> type <FILE NAME 1> <FILE NAME 2> <FILE NAME 3> > <NEW
FILE NAME>
```

Desktops, allows multiple Desktop Screens:

Ref. https://technet.microsoft.com/en-
us/sysinternals/cc817881

Run live option:

```
C:\> "%ProgramFiles%\Internet Explorer\iexplore.exe
"https://live.sysinternals.com/desktops.exe
```

Remote mounting, Read and Read/Write:

```
C:\> net share MyShare_R=c:\<READ ONLY FOLDER>
/GRANT:EVERYONE,READ
```

```
C:\> net share MyShare_RW=c:\<READ/WRITE FOLDER>
/GRANT:EVERYONE,FULL
```

Remote task execution using PSEXEC:

Ref. https://technet.microsoft.com/en-
us/sysinternals/psexec.aspx

```
C:\> psexec.exe \\<TARGET IP ADDRESS> -u <USER NAME> -p
<PASSWORD> /c C:\<PROGRAM>.exe
```

```
C:\> psexec @C:\<TARGET FILE LIST>.txt -u <ADMIN LEVEL
USER NAME> -p <PASSWORD> C:\<PROGRAM>.exe >> C:\<OUTPUT
FILE NAME>.txt
```

```
C:\> psexec.exe @C:\<TARGET FILE LIST>.csv -u <DOMAIN
NAME>\<USER NAME> -p <PASSWORD> /c C:\<PROGRAM>.exe
```

Remote task execution and send output to share:

```
C:\> wmic /node:ComputerName process call create "cmd.exe
/c netstat -an > \\<REMOTE SHARE>\<OUTPUT FILE NAME>.txt"
```

Compare two files for changes:

```
PS C:\> Compare-Object (Get-Content .<LOG FILE NAME
1>.log) -DifferenceObject (Get-Content .<LOG FILE NAME
2>.log)
```

Remote task execution using PowerShell:

```
PS C:\> Invoke-Command -<COMPUTER NAME> {<PS COMMAND>}
```

PowerShell Command Help:

```
PS C:\> Get-Help <PS COMMAND> -full
```

Analyze traffic remotely over ssh:

```
# ssh root@<REMOTE IP ADDRESS OF HOST TO SNIFF> tcpdump -i
any -U -s 0 -w - 'not port 22'
```

Manually add note/data to syslog:

```
# logger "Something important to note in Log"
```

```
# dmesg | grep <COMMENT>
```

Simple read only mounting:

```
# mount -o ro /dev/<YOUR FOLDER OR DRIVE> /mnt
```

Mounting remotely over SSH:

```
# apt-get install sshfs
```

```
# adduser <USER NAME> fuse
```

Log out and log back in.

```
mkdir ~/<WHERE TO MOUNT LOCALLY>
```

```
# sshfs <REMOTE USER NAME>@<REMOTE HOST>:/<REMOTE PATH>
~/<WHERE TO MOUNT LOCALLY>
```

Creating a SMB share in Linux:

```
# useradd -m <NEW USER>
```

```
# passwd <NEW USER>
```

```
# smbpasswd -a <NEW USER>
```

```
# echo [Share] >> /etc/samba/smb.conf
```

```
# echo /<PATH OF FOLDER TO SHARE> >> /etc/samba/smb.conf
```

```
# echo available = yes >> /etc/samba/smb.conf
```

```
# echo valid users = <NEW USER> >> /etc/samba/smb.conf
```

```
# echo read only = no >> /etc/samba/smb.conf
```

```
# echo browsable = yes >> /etc/samba/smb.conf
```

```
# echo public = yes >> /etc/samba/smb.conf
```

```
# echo writable = yes >> /etc/samba/smb.conf
```

```
# service smbd restart
```

Visit share from remote system:

```
> smb:\\<IP ADDRESS OF LINUX SMB SHARE>
```

Copy files to remote system:

```
> scp <FILE NAME> <USER NAME>@<DESTINATION IP
ADDRESS>:/<REMOTE FOLDER>
```

Mount a SMB share to remote system:

```
# mount -t smbfs -o username=<USER NAME> //<SERVER NAME OR
IP ADDRESS>/<SHARE NAME> /mnt/<MOUNT POINT>/
```

Monitor if a website or file is still accessible:

```
# while :; do curl -sSr http://<URL> | head -n 1; sleep
60; done
```

Use Screen to manage multiple shell sessions, list
sessions, create new shell and switch to other shells:

```
# screen
# screen -ls
```

Hit Ctrl-a then c

Hit Ctrl-a then n

Re-attach a screen:

```
# screen -x
```

Start a service that will keep running after logout and
return back to prompt:

```
#nohup ./<COMMAND> > <OUTPUT TO A FILE> &
```

Check list of nohup running jobs:

```
# jobs -l
```

Kill a nohup job:

```
# kill %<JOB NUMBER>
```

Check which command is being used and list all locations:

```
# which <COMMAND NAME>
# which -a <COMMAND NAME>
```

DECODING

HEX CONVERSION

Convert from hex to decimal in Windows:

```
C:\> set /a 0xff
255
PS C:\> 0xff
255
```

Other Basic Math in Windows:

```
C:\> set /a 1+2
3
C:\> set /a 3*(9/4)
6
C:\> set /a (2*5)/2
5
C:\> set /a "32>>3"
4
```

Decode Base64 text in a file:

```
C:\> certutil –decode <BASE64 ENCODED FILE NAME> <DECODED FILE NAME>
```

Decode XOR and search for HTTP:

Ref. https://blog.didierstevens.com/programs/xorsearch/

```
C:\> xorsearch.exe –i –s <INPUT FILE NAME> http
```

Convert from hex to decimal in Linux:

```
# echo "0xff"|wcalc –d
= 255
```

Convert from decimal to hex in Linux:

```
$ echo "255"|wcalc -h
= 0xff
```

Decode HTML Strings:

```
PS C:\> Add-Type -AssemblyName System.Web
PS C:\>
[System.Uri]::UnescapeDataString("HTTP%3a%2f%2fHello%20Wor
ld.com")

HTTP://Hello World.com
```

SNORT RULES

Snort Rules to detect Meterpreter traffic:

Ref. https://blog.didierstevens.com/2015/06/16/metasploit-meterpreter-reverse-https-snort-rule/

```
alert tcp $HOME_NET any -> $EXTERNAL_NET $HTTP_PORTS
(msg:"Metasploit User Agent String";
flow:to_server,established; content:"User-Agent|3a|
Mozilla/4.0 (compatible\; MSIE 6.0\; Windows NT 5.1)|0d
0a|"; http_header; classtype:trojan-activity;
reference:url,blog.didierstevens.com/2015/03/16/quickpost-
metasploit-user-agent-strings/; sid:1618000; rev:1;)

alert tcp $HOME_NET any -> $EXTERNAL_NET $HTTP_PORTS
(msg:"Metasploit User Agent String";
flow:to_server,established; content:"User-Agent|3a|
Mozilla/4.0 (compatible\; MSIE 6.1\; Windows NT)|0d 0a|";
http_header; classtype:trojan-activity;
reference:url,blog.didierstevens.com/2015/03/16/quickpost-
metasploit-user-agent-strings/; sid:1618001; rev:1;)

alert tcp $HOME_NET any -> $EXTERNAL_NET $HTTP_PORTS
(msg:"Metasploit User Agent String";
flow:to_server,established; content:"User-Agent|3a|
Mozilla/4.0 (compatible\; MSIE 7.0\; Windows NT 6.0)|0d
0a|"; http_header; classtype:trojan-activity;
reference:url,blog.didierstevens.com/2015/03/16/quickpost-
metasploit-user-agent-strings/; sid:1618002; rev:1;)

alert tcp $HOME_NET any -> $EXTERNAL_NET $HTTP_PORTS
(msg:"Metasploit User Agent String";
flow:to_server,established; content:"User-Agent|3a|
Mozilla/4.0 (compatible\; MSIE 7.0\; Windows NT 6.0\;
Trident/4.0\; SIMBAR={7DB0F6DE-8DE7-4841-9084-
28FA914B0F2E}\; SLCC1\; .N|0d 0a|"; http_header;
classtype:trojan-activity;
reference:url,blog.didierstevens.com/2015/03/16/quickpost-
metasploit-user-agent-strings/; sid:1618003; rev:1;)

alert tcp $HOME_NET any -> $EXTERNAL_NET $HTTP_PORTS
(msg:"Metasploit User Agent String";
```

```
flow:to_server,established; content:"User-Agent|3a|
Mozilla/4.0 (compatible\; Metasploit RSPEC)|0d 0a|";
http_header; classtype:trojan-activity;
reference:url,blog.didierstevens.com/2015/03/16/quickpost-
metasploit-user-agent-strings/; sid:1618004; rev:1;)

alert tcp $HOME_NET any -> $EXTERNAL_NET $HTTP_PORTS
(msg:"Metasploit User Agent String";
flow:to_server,established; content:"User-Agent|3a|
Mozilla/5.0 (Windows\; U\; Windows NT 5.1\; en-US)
AppleWebKit/525.13 (KHTML, like Gecko) Chrome/4.0.221.6
Safari/525.13|0d 0a|"; http_header; classtype:trojan-
activity;
reference:url,blog.didierstevens.com/2015/03/16/quickpost-
metasploit-user-agent-strings/; sid:1618005; rev:1;)

alert tcp $HOME_NET any -> $EXTERNAL_NET $HTTP_PORTS
(msg:"Metasploit User Agent String";
flow:to_server,established; content:"User-Agent|3a|
Mozilla/5.0 (compatible\; Googlebot/2.1\;
+http://www.google.com/bot.html)|0d 0a|"; http_header;
classtype:trojan-activity;
reference:url,blog.didierstevens.com/2015/03/16/quickpost-
metasploit-user-agent-strings/; sid:1618006; rev:1;)

alert tcp $HOME_NET any -> $EXTERNAL_NET $HTTP_PORTS
(msg:"Metasploit User Agent String";
flow:to_server,established; content:"User-Agent|3a|
Mozilla/5.0 (compatible\; MSIE 10.0\; Windows NT 6.1\;
Trident/6.0)|0d 0a|"; http_header; classtype:trojan-
activity;
reference:url,blog.didierstevens.com/2015/03/16/quickpost-
metasploit-user-agent-strings/; sid:1618007; rev:1;)
```

Snort Rules to detect PSEXEC traffic:

Ref. https://github.com/John-Lin/docker-
snort/blob/master/snortrules-snapshot-2972/rules/policy-
other.rules

```
alert tcp $HOME_NET any -> $HOME_NET [139,445]
(msg:"POLICY-OTHER use of psexec remote administration
tool"; flow:to_server,established; content:"|FF|SMB|A2|";
depth:5; offset:4; content:"|5C
00|p|00|s|00|e|00|x|00|e|00|c|00|s|00|v|00|c"; nocase;
metadata:service netbios-ssn;
reference:url,technet.microsoft.com/en-
```

us/sysinternals/bb897553.aspx; classtype:policy-violation;
sid:24008; rev:1;)

alert tcp $HOME_NET any -> $HOME_NET [139,445]
(msg:"POLICY-OTHER use of psexec remote administration
tool SMBv2"; flow:to_server,established;
content:"|FE|SMB"; depth:8; nocase; content:"|05 00|";
within:2; distance:8;
content:"P|00|S|00|E|00|X|00|E|00|S|00|V|00|C|00|";
fast_pattern:only; metadata:service netbios-ssn;
reference:url,technet.microsoft.com/en-
us/sysinternals/bb897553.aspx[1]; classtype:policy-
violation; sid:30281; rev:1;)

FINGERPRINT DOS/DDOS

Fingerprinting the type of DoS/DDoS:

Ref. https://www.trustwave.com/Resources/SpiderLabs-Blog/PCAP-Files-Are-Great-Arn-t-They--/

Volumetric: Bandwidth consumption

Example, sustaining sending 1Gb of traffic to 10Mb connection

Ref. http://freecode.com/projects/iftop

```
# iftop -n
```

Protocol: Use of specific protocol

Example, SYN Flood, ICMP Flood, UDP flood

```
# tshark -r <FILE NAME>.pcap -q -z io,phs
```

```
# tshark -c 1000 -q -z io,phs
```

```
# tcpdump -tnr $FILE |awk -F '.' '{print
$1"."$2"."$3"."$4}' | sort | uniq -c | sort -n | tail
```

```
# tcpdump -qnn "tcp[tcpflags] & (tcp-syn) != 0"
```

```
# netstat -s
```

Example, isolate one protocol and or remove other protocols

```
# tcpdump -nn not arp and not icmp and not udp
```

```
# tcpdump -nn tcp
```

Resource: State and connection exhaustion

Example, Firewall can handle 10,000 simultaneous connections, and attacker sends 20,000

```
# netstat -n | awk '{print $6}' | sort | uniq -c | sort -
nr | head
```

Application: Layer 7 attacks

Example, HTTP GET flood, for a large image file.

```
# tshark -c 10000 -T fields -e http.host | sort | uniq -c
| sort -r | head -n 10

# tshark -r capture6 -T fields -e http.request.full\_uri |
sort | uniq -c | sort -r | head -n 10c

# tcpdump -n 'tcp[32:4] = 0x47455420'| cut -f 7- -d ":"
```

Example, look for excessive file requests, GIF, ZIP, JPEG, PDF, PNG.

```
# tshark -Y "http contains "ff:d8"" || "http contains
"GIF89a"" || "http contains "\x50\x4B\x03\x04"" || "http
contains\xff\xd8" " || "http contains "%PDF"" || "http
contains "\x89\x50\x4E\x47""
```

Example, Look for web application 'user-agent' pattern of abuse.

```
# tcpdump -c 1000 -Ann | grep -Ei 'user-agent' | sort |
uniq -c | sort -nr | head -10
```

Example, show HTTP Header of requested resources.

```
# tcpdump -i en0 -A -s 500 | grep -i refer
```

Sniff HTTP Headers for signs of repeat abuse:

```
# tcpdump -s 1024 -l -A dst <EXAMPLE.COM>
```

Poison: Layer 2 attacks

Example, ARP poison, race condition DNS, DHCP

```
# tcpdump 'arp or icmp'

# tcpdump -tnr <SAMPLE TRAFFIC FILE>.pcap ARP |awk -F '.'
'{print $1"."$2"."$3"."$4}' | sort | uniq -c | sort -n |
tail

# tshark -r <SAMPLE TRAFFIC FILE>.pcap -q -z io,phs| grep
arp.duplicate-address-detected
```

TOOL SUITES

PREBUILT ISO, VIRTUAL MACHINE AND DISTRIBUTIONS

KALI – Open Source Pentesting Distribution

Ref. https://www.kali.org

SIFT – SANS Investigative Forensics Toolkit

Ref. http://sift.readthedocs.org/

REMNUX – A Linux Toolkit for Reverse-Engineering and Analyzing Malware

Ref. https://remnux.org

OPEN VAS – Open Source vulnerability scanner and manager

Ref. http://www.openvas.org

MOLOCH – Large scale IPv4 packet capturing (PCAP), indexing and database system

Ref. https://github.com/aol/moloch/wiki

SECURITY ONION – Linux distro for intrusion detection, network security monitoring, and log management

Ref. https://security-onion-solutions.github.io/security-onion/

NAGIOS – Network Monitoring, Alerting, Response, and Reporting Tool

Ref. https://www.nagios.org

OSSEC – Scalable, multi-platform, open source Host-based Intrusion Detection System

Ref. http://ossec.github.io

SAMURAI WTF – Pre-configured web pen-testing environment

Ref. http://samurai.inguardians.com

RTIR – Request Tracker for Incident Response

Ref. https://www.bestpractical.com/rtir/

HONEYDRIVE - Pre-configured honeypot software packages

Ref. http://sourceforge.net/projects/honeydrive/

The Enhanced Mitigation Experience Toolkit - helps prevent vulnerabilities in software from being successfully exploited

Ref. https://support.microsoft.com/en-us/kb/2458544

ATTACK SURFACE ANALYZER BY MICROSOFT - Baseline Tool

Ref. https://www.microsoft.com/en-us/download/confirmation.aspx?id=24487

WINDOWS TO GO - USB Portable Windows 8

Ref. https://technet.microsoft.com/en-us/library/hh831833.aspx

WINFE - Windows Forensic Environment on CD/USB

Ref. http://winfe.wordpress.com/

DCEPT - Deploying and detecting use of Active Directory honeytokens

Ref. https://www.secureworks.com/blog/dcept

TAILS - The Amnesic Incognito Live System

Ref. https://tails.boum.org

GRR - Google Rapid Respponse framework focused on remote live forensics

Ref. https://github.com/google/grr

7 INCIDENT MANAGEMENT (CHECKLIST)

INCIDENT RESPONSE CHECKLIST

Note: This section is intended to be an incident response guide. Some tasks may not be relevant, required or appropriate. Please consider your environment before implementing each step or other steps as needed.

IDENTIFICATION TASKS

Acquire a copy of Malicious file(s) for analysis?		
Priority: H/M/L	Effort: H/M/L	Open/Closed
Malicious effects on systems list. Acquire an itemized list of all known changes on computer systems, files, settings, registry, services add/modified/deleted or stop/started.		
Priority: H/M/L	Effort: H/M/L	Open/Closed
Which A/V or malware tools can detect and remove malicious threat?		
Priority: H/M/L	Effort: H/M/L	Open/Closed
Where does malware/attacker exit the network?		
Priority: H/M/L	Effort: H/M/L	Open/Closed
Malicious internal/external sites/connections still active?		
Priority: H/M/L	Effort: H/M/L	Open/Closed
Malware listening on any ports?		
Priority: H/M/L	Effort: H/M/L	Open/Closed
Malware method of original infection, and/or weakness?		
Priority: H/M/L	Effort: H/M/L	Open/Closed
Packet capture of Malware trying to infect others?		
Priority: H/M/L	Effort: H/M/L	Open/Closed

Any packet capture of malware trying to communicate out of network and ID method of ports, IPs, DNS, etc?		
Priority: H/M/L	Effort: H/M/L	Open/Closed

Malware pose threat to any sensitive data (Files, credentials, Intellectual Property, PII, etc?		
Priority: H/M/L	Effort: H/M/L	Open/Closed

What are the DNS entries on an infected system?		
Priority: H/M/L	Effort: H/M/L	Open/Closed

Is it possible to detect the first infected system(s)?		
Priority: H/M/L	Effort: H/M/L	Open/Closed

Has the first systems hard drive been preserved?		
Priority: H/M/L	Effort: H/M/L	Open/Closed

Do any scripts need to be ran on live infected systems?		
Priority: H/M/L	Effort: H/M/L	Open/Closed

Is there a desktop management tool? If so, what reports are available to inventory all systems and statuses?		
Priority: H/M/L	Effort: H/M/L	Open/Closed

List of all infected systems?		
Priority: H/M/L	Effort: H/M/L	Open/Closed

Identify any patching missing with current and/or previous vulnerability scan.		
Priority: H/M/L	Effort: H/M/L	Open/Closed

Look for systems that have stopped reporting into Malware servers for updates, or which ones have stopped going to AV vendors for updates.		
Priority: H/M/L	Effort: H/M/L	Open/Closed

Look for systems that have stopped going to Update server or directly to Microsoft for updates.		

How many systems are still unknown, clear, suspicious, or infected?		
Priority: H/M/L	Effort: H/M/L	Open/Closed
Networking device(s) changes. (Switches, Routers, Firewalls, IPS, NAC, Wi-Fi, etc.).		
Priority: H/M/L	Effort: H/M/L	Open/Closed
Active Directory OU isolation of suspected systems.		
Priority: H/M/L	Effort: H/M/L	Open/Closed
Active Directory - User account restrictions and resets.		
Priority: H/M/L	Effort: H/M/L	Open/Closed
Active Directory policies to prohibit threats from running and/or access.		
Priority: H/M/L	Effort: H/M/L	Open/Closed
Firewall blocks.		
Priority: H/M/L	Effort: H/M/L	Open/Closed
DNS blocks (null route malware site(s)).		
Priority: H/M/L	Effort: H/M/L	Open/Closed
Web filtering blocks.		
Priority: H/M/L	Effort: H/M/L	Open/Closed

Administrative AD Password Changes.		
Priority: H/M/L	Effort: H/M/L	Open/Closed

Local Administrative Password Changes.		
Priority: H/M/L	Effort: H/M/L	Open/Closed

User AD Password Changes.		
Priority: H/M/L	Effort: H/M/L	Open/Closed

Local User Password Changes.		
Priority: H/M/L	Effort: H/M/L	Open/Closed

Service Account Password Changes.		
Priority: H/M/L	Effort: H/M/L	Open/Closed

Push Antivirus updates for detected malware.		
Priority: H/M/L	Effort: H/M/L	Open/Closed

Try multiple antivirus tools.		
Priority: H/M/L	Effort: H/M/L	Open/Closed

What Active Directory GPO policies are set (Logs, Restrictions, etc.)?		
Priority: H/M/L	Effort: H/M/L	Open/Closed

What is the network architecture and how would Malware traverse?		
Priority: H/M/L	Effort: H/M/L	Open/Closed

Are there additional IDS/IPS segments that need coverage to prevent/detect outbreak?		
Priority: H/M/L	Effort: H/M/L	Open/Closed

3rd Party Applications missing patches (Adobe, Java, etc.)?		
Priority: H/M/L	Effort: H/M/L	Open/Closed

Monitor client email for vendor or other business continuity items of interest.		
Priority: H/M/L	Effort: H/M/L	Open/Closed

Monitor RDP sessions on external accessible RDP client system.		
Priority: H/M/L	Effort: H/M/L	Open/Closed

Are there any applications in use that are facilitating the attack? If so, are there alternatives?

Priority: H/M/L	Effort: H/M/L	Open/Closed

Is there a baseline system to review for changes?

Priority: H/M/L	Effort: H/M/L	Open/Closed

Monitor user name variations.

Priority: H/M/L	Effort: H/M/L	Open/Closed

Managing and monitoring tasks.

Priority: H/M/L	Effort: H/M/L	Open/Closed

Review border router logs.

Priority: H/M/L	Effort: H/M/L	Open/Closed

Review VPN (remote access) logs.

Priority: H/M/L	Effort: H/M/L	Open/Closed

Citrix / VMWare or similar logs.

Priority: H/M/L	Effort: H/M/L	Open/Closed

Review accounting server(s) logs and trends of users.

Priority: H/M/L	Effort: H/M/L	Open/Closed

Review AD server logs.

Priority: H/M/L	Effort: H/M/L	Open/Closed

Review Anti-Virus (Malicious Code Services) logs.

Priority: H/M/L	Effort: H/M/L	Open/Closed

Review email abuse notifications and logs.

Priority: H/M/L	Effort: H/M/L	Open/Closed

Review DNS logs.

Priority: H/M/L	Effort: H/M/L	Open/Closed

Review account and policy abuse logs.

Priority: H/M/L	Effort: H/M/L	Open/Closed

Review host firewall logs.

Priority: H/M/L	Effort: H/M/L	Open/Closed

Rebuild all systems in life cycle rebuild plan.		
Priority: H/M/L	Effort: H/M/L	Open/Closed
Synchronize time services across of systems.		
Priority: H/M/L	Effort: H/M/L	Open/Closed
Create incident data repository.		
Priority: H/M/L	Effort: H/M/L	Open/Closed
Consider host based IPS.		
Priority: H/M/L	Effort: H/M/L	Open/Closed
Consider Network Access Control (NAC).		
Priority: H/M/L	Effort: H/M/L	Open/Closed
3rd Party internal/external security and perimeter security tools and assessment services.		
Priority: H/M/L	Effort: H/M/L	Open/Closed

Malware Presence on the System:	
Runs in memory only.	Yes|No|Unknown|N/A
Runs out of registry.	Yes|No|Unknown|N/A
Artifacts on disk.	Yes|No|Unknown|N/A
Disk file presence hidden, stored in unallocated, free/slack space or encrypted.	Yes|No|Unknown|N/A
Has no icon.	Yes|No|Unknown|N/A
Has no description or company name.	Yes|No|Unknown|N/A
Unsigned Microsoft images.	Yes|No|Unknown|N/A
Are packed and likely encrypted.	Yes|No|Unknown|N/A
Suspicious DLLs or services.	Yes|No|Unknown|N/A
Backups and swaps itself in and out in place of real file.	Yes|No|Unknown|N/A
Stays alive working in file pairs.	Yes|No|Unknown|N/A
Found in embedded devices, industrial controls and IOT.	Yes|No|Unknown|N/A
Malware Activities	
Downloads new code/functionality.	Yes|No|Unknown|N/A
Leverages pivot system(s) and network path(s) to exit the victim network including VPN/Dial-Up, HTTP/HTTPS, and other standard or non-standard services and ports.	Yes|No|Unknown|N/A
Ability to leverage mobile devices and other removable media.	Yes|No|Unknown|N/A
Ability to detect and utilize authenticated web proxies.	Yes|No|Unknown|N/A
Morphs on victim client system.	Yes|No|Unknown|N/A
Contains red herring (misleading/distracting) features depending on the environment it detects.	Yes|No|Unknown|N/A
Ability to traverse all known operating systems.	Yes|No|Unknown|N/A
Ability to move into embedded devices.	Yes|No|Unknown|N/A
Malware Capabilities	
Ability to conduct most Windows based Active Directory commands.	Yes|No|Unknown|N/A
Ability to upload and download files/payloads.	Yes|No|Unknown|N/A
Can use built-in services or purpose built malware for needed services.	Yes|No|Unknown|N/A
Has several persistent features, making the malware highly resilient	Yes|No|Unknown|N/A

to A/V defenses.	
Ability to brute force.	Yes|No|Unknown|N/A
Ability to DoS/DDoS tools.	Yes|No|Unknown|N/A
Ability to steal and/or pass the hash.	Yes|No|Unknown|N/A
Ability to conduct credential harvesting.	Yes|No|Unknown|N/A
Privilege escalation capability.	Yes|No|Unknown|N/A
Ransomware or like capability.	Yes|No|Unknown|N/A
Self-Destruct mode, including destructive methods.	Yes|No|Unknown|N/A
Anti memory forensics.	Yes|No|Unknown|N/A
Is sandbox aware and virtual machine aware.	Yes|No|Unknown|N/A
Apply software patch to prevent other malware infection	Yes|No|Unknown|N/A
C2 techniques: DNS, HTTP, HTTPS, stegonagraphy, cloud, TOR, online code, etc.	Yes|No|Unknown|N/A
One time install/detonation	Yes|No|Unknown|N/A
Communicates in no predictable patterns including short and long-term sleep techniques.	Yes|No|Unknown|N/A
Makes use of compromised CA, in order to hide communications.	Yes|No|Unknown|N/A
Time zone and IP Geo aware.	Yes|No|Unknown|N/A
Makes use of well-established commercial compromised web sites for C2, i.e. Dropbox, Gmail, etc.	Yes|No|Unknown|N/A

8 SECURITY INCIDENT IDENTIFICATION (Schema)

VOCABULARY FOR EVENTS RECORDING AND INCIDENT SHARING (VERIS)

GENERAL

Ref. http://veriscommunity.net/

Use this template to identify threats uniformly:

incident_id
#

security_incident
Confirmed, Suspected, False positive, Near miss, No

confidence
High, Medium, Low, None

victim.employee_count
#

timeline.unit
Unknown, NA, Seconds, Minutes, Hours, Days, Weeks, Months, Years, Never

impact.overall_rating
Unknown, Insignificant, Distracting, Painful, Damaging, Catastrophic

impact.loss.variety
Asset and fraud, Brand damage, Business disruption, Operating costs, Legal and regulatory, Competitive advantage, Response and recovery

impact.loss.rating
Unknown, Major, Moderate, Minor, None

discovery_method

Unknown, Ext – actor disclosure, Ext – fraud detection, Ext – monitoring service, Ext – customer, Ext – unrelated party, Ext – audit, Ext – unknown, Int – antivirus, Int – incident response, Int – financial audit, Int – fraud detection, Int – HIDS, Int – IT audit, Int – log review, Int – NIDS, Ext – law enforcement, Int – security alarm, Int – reported by user, Int – unknown, Other

targeted

Unknown, Opportunistic, Targeted, NA

cost_corrective_action

Unknown, Simple and cheap, Difficult and expensive, Something in-between

country

Unknown, Two Letter, Other

iso_currency_code

AED, AFN, ALL, AMD, ANG, AOA, ARS, AUD, AWG, AZN, BAM, BBD, BDT, BGN, BHD, BIF, BMD, BND, BOB, BRL, BSD, BTN, BWP, BYR, BZD, CAD, CDF, CHF, CLP, CNY, COP, CRC, CUC, CUP, CVE, CZK, DJF, DKK, DOP, DZD, EGP, ERN, ETB, EUR, FJD, FKP, GBP, GEL, GGP, GHS, GIP, GMD, GNF, GTQ, GYD, HKD, HNL, HRK, HTG, HUF, IDR, ILS, IMP, INR, IQD, IRR, ISK, JEP, JMD, JOD, JPY, KES, KGS, KHR, KMF, KPW, KRW, KWD, KYD, KZT, LAK, LBP, LKR, LRD, LSL, LTL, LVL, LYD, MAD, MDL, MGA, MKD, MMK, MNT, MOP, MRO, MUR, MVR, MWK, MXN, MYR, MZN, NAD, NGN, NIO, NOK, NPR, NZD, OMR, PAB, PEN, PGK, PHP, PKR, PLN, PYG, QAR, RON, RSD, RUB, RWF, SAR, SBD, SCR, SDG, SEK, SGD, SHP, SLL, SOS, SPL, SRD, STD, SVC, SYP, SZL, THB, TJS, TMT, TND, TOP, TRY, TTD, TVD, TWD, TZS, UAH, UGX, USD, UYU, UZS, VEF, VND, VUV, WST, XAF, XCD, XDR, XOF, XPF, YER, ZAR, ZMK, ZWD

actor.x.motive
Unknown, NA, Espionage, Fear, Financial, Fun, Grudge, Ideology, Convenience, Other

actor.external.variety
Unknown, Activist, Auditor, Competitor, Customer, Force majeure, Former employee, Nation-state, Organized crime, Acquaintance, State-affiliated, Terrorist, Unaffiliated, Other

actor.internal.variety
Unknown, Auditor, Call center, Cashier, End-user, Executive, Finance, Helpdesk, Human resources, Maintenance, Manager, Guard, Developer, System admin, Other

action.malware.variety
Unknown, Adware, Backdoor, Brute force, Capture app data, Capture stored data, Client-side attack, Click fraud, C2, Destroy data, Disable controls, DoS, Downloader, Exploit vuln, Export data, Packet sniffer, Password dumper, Ram scraper, Ransomware, Rootkit, Scan network, Spam, Spyware/Keylogger, SQL injection, Adminware, Worm, Other

action.malware.vector
Unknown, Direct install, Download by malware, Email autoexecute, Email link, Email attachment, Instant messaging, Network propagation, Remote injection, Removable media, Web drive-by, Web download, Other

action.hacking.variety
Unknown, Abuse of functionality, Brute force, Buffer overflow, Cache poisoning, Session prediction, CSRF, XSS, Cryptanalysis, DoS, Footprinting, Forced browsing, Format string attack, Fuzz testing, HTTP request smuggling, HTTP request splitting, HTTP response smuggling, HTTP Response Splitting, Integer overflows, LDAP injection, Mail command injection, MitM, Null byte injection, Offline cracking, OS commanding, Path traversal, RFI, Reverse engineering, Routing detour, Session fixation, Session replay, Soap array abuse, Special element injection, SQLi, SSI injection, URL redirector abuse, Use of backdoor or C2, Use of stolen creds, XML attribute blowup, XML entity expansion, XML external entities, XML injection, XPath injection, XQuery injection, Virtual machine escape, Other

action.hacking.vector
Unknown, 3rd party desktop, Backdoor or C2, Desktop sharing, Physical access, Command shell, Partner, VPN, Web application, Other

action.social.variety
Unknown, Baiting, Bribery, Elicitation, Extortion, Forgery, Influence, Scam, Phishing, Pretexting, Propaganda, Spam, Other

action.social.vector
Unknown, Documents, Email, In-person, IM, Phone, Removable media, SMS, Social media, Software, Website, Other

action.social.target
Unknown, Auditor, Call center, Cashier, Customer, End-user, Executive, Finance, Former employee, Helpdesk, Human resources, Maintenance, Manager, Partner, Guard, Developer, System admin, Other

action.misuse.variety
Unknown, Knowledge abuse, Privilege abuse, Embezzlement, Data mishandling, Email misuse, Net misuse, Illicit content, Unapproved workaround, Unapproved hardware, Unapproved software, Other

action.misuse.vector
Unknown, Physical access, LAN access, Remote access, Non-corporate, Other

action.physical.variety
Unknown, Assault, Sabotage, Snooping, Surveillance, Tampering, Theft, Wiretapping, Connection, Other

action.physical.location
Unknown, Partner facility, Partner vehicle, Personal residence, Personal vehicle, Public facility, Public vehicle, Victim secure area, Victim work area, Victim public area, Victim grounds, Other

action.physical.vector
Unknown, Privileged access, Visitor privileges, Bypassed controls, Disabled controls, Uncontrolled location, Other

action.error.variety
Unknown, Classification error, Data entry error, Disposal error, Gaffe, Loss, Maintenance error, Misconfiguration, Misdelivery, Misinformation, Omission, Physical accidents, Capacity shortage, Programming error, Publishing error, Malfunction, Other

action.error.vector
Unknown, Random error, Carelessness, Inadequate personnel, Inadequate processes, Inadequate technology, Other

action.environmental.variety
Unknown, Deterioration, Earthquake, EMI, ESD, Temperature, Fire, Flood, Hazmat, Humidity, Hurricane, Ice, Landslide, Lightning, Meteorite, Particulates, Pathogen, Power failure, Tornado, Tsunami, Vermin, Volcano, Leak, Wind, Other

asset.variety
Unknown, S – Authentication, S – Backup, S – Database, S – DHCP, S – Directory, S – DCS, S – DNS, S – File, S – Log, S – Mail, S – Mainframe, S – Payment switch, S – POS controller, S – Print, S – Proxy, S – Remote access, S – SCADA, S – Web application, S – Code repository, S – VM host, S – Other N – Access reader, N – Camera, N – Firewall, N – HSM, N – IDS, N – Broadband, N – PBX, N – Private WAN, N – PLC, N – Public WAN, N – RTU, N – Router or switch, N – SAN, N – Telephone, N – VoIP adapter, N – LAN, N – WLAN, N – Other U – Auth token, U – Desktop, U – Laptop, U – Media, U – Mobile phone, U – Peripheral, U – POS terminal, U – Tablet, U – Telephone, U – VoIP phone, U – Other T – ATM, T – PED pad, T – Gas terminal, T – Kiosk, T – Other M – Tapes, M – Disk media, M – Documents, M – Flash drive, M – Disk drive, M – Smart card, M – Payment card, M – Other P – System admin, P – Auditor, P – Call center, P – Cashier, P – Customer, P – Developer, P – End-user, P – Executive, P – Finance, P – Former employee, P – Guard, P – Helpdesk, P – Human resources, P – Maintenance, P – Manager, P – Partner, P – Other

asset.accessibility
Unknown, External, Internal, Isolated, NA

asset.ownership
Unknown, Victim, Employee, Partner, Customer, NA

asset.management
Unknown, Internal, External, NA

asset.hosting
Unknown, Internal, External shared, External dedicated, External, NA

asset.cloud
Unknown, Hypervisor, Partner application, Hosting governance, Customer attack, Hosting

attribute.confidentiality.data_disclosure
Unknown, Yes, Potentially, No

attribute.confidentiality.data.variety
Unknown, Credentials, Bank, Classified, Copyrighted, Medical, Payment, Personal, Internal, System, Secrets, Other

attribute.confidentiality.state
Unknown, Stored, Stored encrypted, Stored unencrypted, Transmitted, Transmitted encrypted, Transmitted unencrypted, Processed

attribute.integrity.variety
Unknown, Created account, Hardware tampering, Alter behavior, Fraudulent transaction, Log tampering, Misappropriation, Misrepresentation, Modify configuration, Modify privileges, Modify data, Software installation, Other

attribute.availability.variety
Unknown, Destruction, Loss, Interruption, Degradation, Acceleration, Obscuration, Other

COURSE OF ACTION

Structured Threat Information eXpression (STIX™) (Adapted)

Ref. https://stixproject.github.io

coa.type
Blocking, Redirecting, Hardening, Patching, Rebuilding, Monitoring, Other

coa.impact
Insignificant, Distracting, Painful, Damaging, Catastrophic, Unknown

coa.efficacy
Not Effective, Somewhat Effective, Mostly Effective, Completely Effective, NA

coa.stage
Prepare, Remedy, Response, Recovered

coa.hosting
Unknown, Internal, External shared, External dedicated, External, NA

coa.objective
Detect, Deny, Disrupt, Degrade, Deceive, Destroy

KILL CHAIN MAPPING

GATHER DATA FOR MAPPING KILL CHAIN

Ref.
http://www.lockheedmartin.com/content/dam/lockheed/data/co
rporate/documents/LM-White-Paper-Intel-Driven-Defense.pdf

Phase	Identified evidence, artifact, info, or intel	Course of Action
Active Reconnaissance		Detect, Deny, Disrupt, Degrade, Deceive, Destroy
Weaponization and Customization		Detect, Deny, Disrupt, Degrade, Deceive, Destroy
Delivery		Detect, Deny, Disrupt, Degrade, Deceive, Destroy
Exploitation		Detect, Deny, Disrupt, Degrade, Deceive, Destroy
Installation		Detect, Deny, Disrupt, Degrade, Deceive, Destroy
Command & Control (C2)		Detect, Deny, Disrupt, Degrade, Deceive, Destroy
Action on Objectives		Detect, Deny, Disrupt, Degrade, Deceive, Destroy

PRIORITIZED DEFENDED ASSET LIST (PDAL)

GATHER DATA AND PRIORITIZE ASSETS TO DEFEND

Asset:			
Location:		Criticality:	
Description:		Vulnerability:	
Purpose:		Recoverability:	
Time Prioritized:		Ranking:	
Priority:		I	

Asset:			
Location:		Criticality:	
Description:		Vulnerability:	
Purpose:		Recoverability:	
Time Prioritized:		Ranking:	
Priority:		II	

Asset:			
Location:		Criticality:	
Description:		Vulnerability:	
Purpose:		Recoverability:	
Time Prioritized:		Ranking:	
Priority:		III	

SCRATCH PAD

SCRATCH PAD

10 INDEX (A–Z)

Made in United States
North Haven, CT
16 January 2022

14859409R00074